I Laffed Till I Cried

I LAFFED
Till I Cried
Thirty-Six Years of Marriage to Jerry Lewis

By *Patti Lewis*
With *Sarah Anne Coleman* • *Foreword by Lorraine Hope Caldwell*

WRS
PUBLISHING

A Division of WRS Group, Inc.
Waco, Texas

First published in the United States of America in 1993 by WRS Publishing,
A Division of WRS Group, Inc., 701 N. New Road, Waco, Texas 76710
Book design by Kenneth Turbeville

10 9 8 7 6 5 4 3 2 1

Library of Congress Cataloging-in-Publication Data

Lewis, Patti, 1921-
    I laffed till I cried : thirty-six years of marriage to Jerry Lewis / by Patti
Lewis, with Sarah Coleman ; foreword by Lorraine Hope Caldwell.
        p.   cm.
    ISBN 1-56796-035-9 : $19.95
    1. Lewis, Jerry, 1926-   . 2. Lewis, Patti, 1921-   .
3. Comedians—United States—Biography. I. Coleman, Sarah Jepson.
PN2287.L435L48   1993
791.43'028'092—dc20
    [B]   93-25671
                                                                  CIP

Dedication

To my sons, Gary, Ron, Scott, Chris, Anthony, and Joseph
To their wives and my grandchildren

And to my brother, Joe.

Today may be better than yesterday,
but never as good as tomorrow!

Foreword

When I was asked to write the foreword to Patti's book, I was both pleased and flattered: pleased because it gives me a chance to say something about Patti that she would not say about herself, and flattered because Patti wanted me to do it.

Patti Lewis has been my close friend, confidante, and someone I have considered more a sister than a friend for over thirty years. We have shared some wonderfully happy times during that period, and have seen each other through some equally miserable ones. She was always there for me during both the good and the bad, as I hope I have been for her. She is the kind of friend who is generous with her time, thoughtful gifts, and her friendship.

We have watched our children grow from infancy, through school, weddings, grandchildren, trials, tribulations… and celebrations.

Those who do not know Patti well may criticize her for not "telling all" to the supermarket scandal rags in retaliation for the humiliation she has endured because of some of the articles about her family. Patti has the ability to turn the other cheek, to forgive—not because she is weak, but because she truly lives her religion. When she prays the Lord's Prayer and says, "forgive us our trespasses as we forgive others," it is not just words by rote, but a sincere plea to God… and one she lives by. She fully intends to maintain her dignity, and I know so well that it has not always been easy.

When Patti was married to Jerry, life was Hollywood

parties, glamorous gowns, beautiful jewelry, a full household staff in the Bel Air mansion, and everything that accompanies marriage to a celebrity. With it all, Patti was—and still is—one of the most down-to-earth, genuine human beings I have ever known. I can still remember Jerry saying many, many years ago, "If I buy Patti a new refrigerator, she will ask if I made sure to get the Blue Chip stamps." She was devoted to her six boys and not much interested in lunching at the "in" places to see and be seen. She bowled on a team weekly with other mothers. It was one of her favorite outside activities—much more fun than the glitzy affairs. She was president of a large Catholic charity organization, a member of many others.

Few are aware of Patti's impressive credentials. She not only had an admirable career before marriage, but remains vice president and partner in P.J. Productions, which has produced twenty-five major motion pictures, including *Rock-A-Bye Baby*, *Cinderfella*, and *The Nutty Professor*.

She was executive producer and manager of the band, Gary Lewis and the Playboys, for several years. The group recorded more than twenty albums and had ten top singles.

She has been a hostess for the telethons and has worked with the Neuro-Muscular Disease Center for UCLA. She is a Patron of the Arts of the Vatican Museum and a member of A.F.T.R.A., the Society of Singers, and other prestigious organizations.

Patti has guested on "Oprah Winfrey," "Donahue," "Hour of Power," Trinity Network, "Geraldo," "Larry King Live," "The Today Show," and CBN, and has appeared with Dale Evans. If Jerry gives himself away for kids, she gives generously of herself for people and organizations. Her focus is always on the goal of the organization, not on being in the spotlight.

When my youngest son was married several years ago in Northern California, Patti flew up with me and my family for the wedding and a three-day celebration. A few days after we returned home, Patti came over with 160 photos of the weekend. I now have a scrapbook of those memories. She also gave me the negatives so I could have a full set made for the bride and groom. It was typical of Patti to think of that, and it is a gift never to be forgotten.

There are times when weeks go by without our getting together, although we frequently talk on the telephone. But I know that, should I need her, she is just there... and I hope she knows that I will be there for her, ready to return the friendship she exemplifies.

Lorraine Hope Caldwell
Los Angeles, California

Introduction

A friend pulled up a chair and together we sat in my garden. Rather intensely she asked, "Are you trying to live on your memories?" She hesitated, then continued, "It can be devastating, you know. Trying to rely on past experiences keeps a person on the edge. Inner resources can become warmed-over blessings and lead to sentimentality. Sentimental journeys may be counter-productive and at best, unfulfilling."

Her words echoed in my mind for a long time. Reaching back to write this book has touched untold emotions and split countless nerve endings. At times I have felt like half a person looking for the rest of me. I have experienced frustration, anger, and pain. Yet on other occasions, I have been so overjoyed and excited that every trace of self-pity has fled.

In my long hours of searching through boxes of yesterdays, sorting hundreds of pictures, reviews, journals, and clippings, I have felt almost like a badminton shuttlecock, fluttering back and forth in an emotional battering game. I have contrasted what was, and, with anxiety, perceived what might have been. But through it all I have made a stunning discovery—the past is valuable if one uses it as a guidepost, but dangerous if it becomes a hitching post.

This book is not my hitching post. Although the past is never far behind, I'm moving forward by looking back—back through an abusive childhood, back through a developing career with Jimmy Dorsey's orchestra, back to raising six sons, and back to being married to the world's "biggest goof." In the process I have found myself making an extreme effort to suppress melancholy thoughts and nourish fond remembrances.

It is easy to judge others by their actions and ourselves by our intentions. I sincerely believe my action in writing this book is good, as have been the intentions during the many years I have considered the project.

It had to be more than fate that brought Jerry and me together. We shared so many similarities. His grandparents came through Ellis Island. My parents steamed past the same Statue of Liberty into immigrant processing. When we met we were both performers. We had both been lonely as children. Maybe these were the common denominators that tied us together so quickly. What followed was thirty-six years of breaks—good breaks and tough ones, then the toughest of all, our ultimate breakup. (One tabloid headline from that time still stings— ANOTHER HOLLYWOOD WIFE ON THE JUNK HEAP!)

Education is the process of moving from cocky sureness—such as I had when I married Jerry—to thoughtful uncertainty. That uncertainty, as to just how securely we were tied, I have pondered in my heart for a long time.

Beverly Hills and Bel Air have two kinds of homes: those which have problems and those which will have them. Hollywood is a symbol of success and sadness. The Lewis family was no exception. No one knows better than I that all that glitters is not gold.

I have often been asked what makes happiness. I must simply answer that I'm not sure if it is celebrity status, autographs, yachts, indefinables, smiles, wardrobe, visibility, laughs, magnificent homes, burgeoning bank accounts, or none of the above! A gossip columnist used to say that the secret of a Hollywood wife is to be content with what you get—so get plenty! I succeeded in getting plenty—of memories.

My memories are mostly kind and gentle, honest and clear. But they are also memories of having ultimately to strip every dependence but faith, while suppressing anxious thoughts every day. I learned again that faith—the kind of true faith that is not constricting or limiting, but liberating and life-changing—is bigger than my fear.

I was trapped by so-called success, while living with a man who was rarely the father or husband our family needed, yet who was gifted with a talent to make the rest of the world laugh.

I have stated many times since our separation and divorce that I will always care for Jerry. Thirty-six years was a major segment in the lives of us both. With the clarity of hindsight I recognize and appreciate the wonderful times and great moments we shared. I will always love Jerry, but I could not live with the man he had become.

In this book I have deliberately chosen to be positive because I've never been enamored with those who play the blame game. A friend gave me a card that reinforces my belief.

Blame never affirms, it assaults.
Blame never restores, it wounds.
Blame never solves, it complicates.
Blame never unites, it separates.
Blame never smiles, it frowns.
Blame never forgives, it rejects.
Blame never forgets, it remembers.
Blame rarely builds, it destroys.

My desire is to build a future on the joys and sorrows of the past. Failure is never final; success is never certain. We learn from both to move ahead and start again.

I realize that I am exposing our lives to the world. In so doing, my honest desire is for you to walk with me down history's streets, and to walk with understanding, remembering there is always a world behind the words. I hope the trip will be stimulating, entertaining, and possibly a little rewarding.

I am not what I used to be, nor have I achieved what I

want to be. But I have learned to focus on what I have rather than on what I may have lost. Each day I am more convinced that good memories are irreplaceable. Faith, family, and loyal friends are life's enduring treasures.

Who will buy my memories?
A journey of many years.
Sunshine and shadows, joy and pain
Hope, laughter, and tears.

Who would want to peer inside,
And read what most forget?
Or care that I'm replacing hurt
With hope and not regret.

Who will buy these memories?
Collected, compiled, pictured, too.
Those, I think, who have "laffed till they've cried."
I am glad one of those is you!

Chapter 1

Our meeting was unique. We were both fledgling entertainers, both making our mark. We met backstage. I was wearing platform shoes, had wire rollers in my hair, and was carrying an awkward makeup case. Jerry was decked out in a zoot suit, suspenders to hold up his pants, and thick, rubber-soled shoes.

I first noticed the space between his front teeth, the mole on his chin, and his shiny black, pompadoured hair. I thought he was Italian. (At times, he did too!)

That night Jerry was the intermission act, doing pantomime to records of Frank Sinatra and Danny Kaye, as well as operas and impersonators. My band was to follow him.

Later in the evening we met at Papa Joe's for pizza. Jerry arrived with lipstick on his collar. Being the comedian he was, he soon conned his way out of that and I found myself laughing with him.

Had I but known it, the smeared lipstick was a prologue to the future.

A few nights later we walked to a nearby park, sat on a bench, and talked. After a little while, a vagrant wandered by and offered Jerry a cheap, homemade ring for fifty cents. Jerry paid him and presented the ring to me. It was a wonderful moment. (I still have that tarnished piece of memorabilia tucked in my jewelry box.)

Soon after this I walked into the theater and found, hanging over the makeup table in my dressing room, a pair of soap baby shoes and the words, "Let's fill these," scrawled in lipstick across the mirror.

Remembering that day is like bumping against the past, and feeling as if someone turned on all the lights in my life. Things would never be the same again.

Although we were young, we were married that fall in a hotel room, under the traditional Jewish canopy—the *huppah*. Until then it had never entered my besotted mind that Jerry might be something other than Italian.

The fact that Jerry was Jewish was difficult for me to assimilate, since I had been brought up to fear anyone who was Jewish. (As a little girl I would run as fast as I could past a Jewish-owned corner grocery store.) There was not much religion in my home, except for Mass on Sunday and a tiny statue of St. Anthony in our apartment. My mother, who had been sixteen when I was born, worked in a factory and said little about any kind of faith. Yet somehow I had learned to fear Jews.

Now I was marrying one.

Our wedding was simple and somewhat confusing, as I understood so little of what was transpiring. The only thing I knew for sure was that I could not live without the man at my side. It was a welcome relief to hear Jerry say "I do." There was no doubt for me. My "I do" meant a future of cooking and sewing, washing clothes and dishes, and obeying my husband. That was the way little girls were brought up to be in my neighborhood.

I remember Jerry's mom and dad and two aunts were witnesses to the ceremony. They each held one post of the *huppah* under which we stood. We shared a cup of wine and the event was over. Only Jerry and I knew that I was pregnant—a secret we shared for many years. Nothing overshadowed our joy, not even our parents' lack of enthusiasm for the union, which was based on our differing faiths.

My mother made a scene when she learned that I had married Jerry. But when she saw him again, she couldn't help laughing at his antics. He had started performing his routines when he was five years old and they were well-rehearsed by the time he was vying for my affection and that of my mother. He won both of us over.

Mother was concerned that I would not remain Catholic, so much so that she gave me her tiny St. Anthony statue for my own home. I felt it was a sacrifice. She probably felt it was an insurance policy to help me "keep the faith"—her faith.

Gary's birth was wonderful. The birth of a son in Jewish families is special. Jerry arrived after I had been wheeled out of the delivery room, and told me we had a boy. Jerry's family came to the hospital for the *bris*, the circumcision ceremony. However, the day I went home, Jerry was working in Baltimore, quite a distance from New Jersey, where our first, postage-stamp-sized apartment was located.

Having to call a cab myself to take our little baby boy home was an experience of the cold chill of isolation. In retrospect, I have empathy for that old Jewish grocer in Detroit who must have also had lonely feelings when unkind neighbors froze him out of their lives.

I had a lot to learn about diverse faiths and cultures.

By then, I had developed a strange kind of fear of a certain rabbi—Jerry's grandfather. He was one of a long line of rabbis until his son, Jerry's father, broke tradition and went into show business. One could see his disappointment at this as the frail, tiny man lived his life in a strict kosher home with rules for every phase of living. He spent Saturdays in the synagogue and read the *Talmud* by the hour.

The first time Jerry and I took our son to visit him in his Brooklyn apartment, the place was full of relatives. As if it had happened only yesterday, I remember the slap of his hand against the old wooden chair as, with sparks in his eyes, he thundered, "You're not fooling me. I knew you were a *shiska* from the first day we met!"

I felt reduced to a lump of worthlessness. The wise old man knew I was a Gentile! But Rabbi-grandfather was not finished.

He pierced Jerry with a look as if nailing a proclamation to a wall and said, "Now look at my grandson. She loves him. She takes care of him. He's happy. All this before God is small. Love like theirs is big."

In that moment something leaped within my heart. In a few precious words he had broken down barriers and prejudices, and filled that room with God's true love. Could it be that the God "they" worshipped was the same one Christians worshipped? I had a lot to learn, but truth was pouring out of that rabbi and my love for him and his God became very real that afternoon. Love overcame prayer shawls, rituals, and dietary laws. His love seemed to encompass the world. I wondered if it were possible that someday I could become heir to such unconditional love.

Those early years were tough and triumphant. Jerry was rising quickly as a star. I felt like a shadow-player when I watched him on the stage. But I was very proud of him.

When Gary was two and a half years old, we adopted our second son, Ron. A physician friend had told us about him and we were both so excited. The doctor called to say the baby had been born at 7:30—just the time I had awakened that morning!—and I dashed to the hospital to see him. He was so sleepy, but the most gorgeous towhead I had ever seen. From the first moment, I knew he was *ours*.

Jerry's pride in me, Gary, and Ron, our second son, came in the form of a little booklet he made for me in 1951, when our marriage was seven years old. It was my most cherished publication. The booklet will never be on the *New York Times* list of bestsellers, but its contents are his recollections of our meeting and time together. It is another stored memory, frozen in time. He wrote:

JUST 'CAUSE I LOVE HER
by JERRY LEWIS
July 4, 1951
I DEDICATE THIS TO MY INSPIRATION **PATTI**

When I stepped out of the cab that Thursday in August, 1944, I thought there couldn't be a happier guy. I was to appear in Detroit that week, at the Downtown Theater, one of the better vaude houses. Besides, I was to earn all of four hundred dollars, and at that time it was a small fortune. Naturally, after struggling for a long while, I was now as happy as a man could be. I didn't think it possible to be any happier. I was dead wrong.

I paid the driver, opened the stage door, walked in, and sat down. I don't think I sat longer than ten minutes. It seemed ten years. I guess it was because there wasn't anyone to talk to. I thought I'd go outside for some coffee, (really hoping that someone would recognize me from the pictures out front) and as I took a few steps toward the door, it opened. All I could see was a large makeup box at the end of an adorable arm. The arm belonged to a little Italian singer, who looked as though she had just carried the whole band on her back from a one-nighter in Hershey, Pennsylvania.

Her pigtails weren't as pretty or as smartly combed as she would have liked them to be. I didn't know why I felt funny. I guess it was because the happiness I had felt minutes before was now mild compared to the joy and happiness I knew I would one day share with the little band singer who looked at me as if I were some Detroit jerk waiting for an autograph...

The only sound in the cold corridor was the patter of her little size-six, gum-soled loafers. I remember watching her walk down the long hallway to her dressing room. I wanted so to call out and tell her I was an actor, too, and that we'd be working together that week. Just as I was about to do so, an elderly gentleman demanded my attention. I turned to him and listened as he spoke his piece. It was the first time I remembered my heart pounding while giving light...

Well... it was time for rehearsal, so off I went to my dressing room... I took the first landing real

slow, hoping she would be on that floor. No luck...
I did the same on the second and third floors, and
still no luck. I couldn't go to the fourth because I
had already reached my own room, but at least I
knew she was on the floor above me. I tried so hard
to find something missing, but I had everything...
Kleenex, etc... so I figured I'd see her on stage.

The show was on. I never liked Spanish music,
but for the first time, "Bim Bam Boom" sounded
like Beethoven's Fifth. I had never known this
excitement before. It wasn't physical... it wasn't
loneliness... it wasn't something I had talked myself
into... I know now... I had fallen in love.

I would work every show to the wing as well as
to the audience, hoping she would be watching. I
found out much later, she had been, without my
knowing. I guess that's the way girls are. Time went
on... all of three days... I hadn't eaten... I hadn't
slept... I didn't feel right... No, I was okay with the
draft, despite my punctured eardrum... All I needed
was some sort of encouragement from the little lady
I thought of as 'My Princess.'

When she accepted my invitation to dinner, I
felt better than a thirty-five dollar act when they are
booked to headline the Palace. We went to a
restaurant next door to the theater. I said I thought
it would be wise not to go too far and possibly miss
the show, but I'm almost sure she knew I didn't
have enough to take her to a classy joint. She made
me feel as though the chicken salad I bought for her
was a rare New York steak... She didn't eat it,
though... I thought at the time she didn't feel good.
When she later married me, I knew that that night
she felt the same as I.

The only time that week my heart was hurt was
the day I met her mom and I said, "I'm going to
marry your daughter." Her mom laughed at me... I
had devoted my whole life to making people laugh...
but this was the one time I wished I wasn't funny.

I was as thrilled when we rode through the park in a cab, as the day I first put on long pants. When I kissed her and told her I loved her, she looked into my eyes and I knew my life was first beginning. I said goodnight and she ran into the house like a happy but frightened puppy.

I'm afraid I'm not eloquent enough to express the joy and contentment I experienced riding back to the hotel that night.

The next day we boarded a N.Y.-bound train. When we stopped at Syracuse, My Princess was to leave me. Detroit to Syracuse is nine hours, and in that short span of time I think I said, "I love you" once, and sighed the rest of the time away. When the man with the brass buttons and chevrons on his sleeve called, "Syracuse," I was certain it was the voice of the devil. I walked slowly but firmly to the platform to help the lovely lady off the train... she cried and said goodbye... I wanted to cry... but I was a man of course... but when the porter closed the door... I became a kid again.

The letters I received were as important to me as was medicine to a sick man. Time moved slowly... We would meet in New Haven, New York, Boston, whenever we could get away. Our love was so wonderful we thought that surely we were the first to love. The only thing we dreamt about was to get married... and we did.

We had nothing but our love...

She was playing the Capitol Theater... I sat in the last row, opening day, with my fingers crossed, and my heart crying, "Why ain't I up there, making her dependent on me?" I wasn't jealous... I just wanted to do big things so she'd be proud of me... it was on that day I vowed I would play there and every other important place, only for her. Little did I know that it would be her guidance and faith that would enable me to keep my promise to myself.

Months passed and I was called to the hospital

to see my Princess before she went to the delivery room. I just made it in time to say, "I love you," then they wheeled her in. The thirty minutes I spent waiting were horrible but this was one father who knew God would listen to his prayers and take care of the little lady who was so necessary to his existence. The huge doors swung open... and there she was... I dreaded asking if she was all right, but the smile on the doctor's face assured me that all was okay. "Your baby weighs seven eleven," the doctor said as if he were announcing a ball game and not concerned at all about torturing my lady.

I wasn't allowed to put more than one dozen roses in her room, but she didn't even notice them, so it was okay. All she could say was, "I gave you a son." From the day of his birth, the two of them helped make a small-time actor a real big guy, if not in the eyes of the public, at least in the eyes of the family to whom I dedicate my life. Patti, My Princess, Gary, my son, Ronnie, my boy...

The rest of the story is common knowledge... today I am doing television, pictures, nightclubs, personal appearances, eight shows a day... of course with the guy I owe half my life to... So it's natural for you to wonder how I have time to sit and write something like this... I think the reason I make time is... just 'cause I love her.

There were many times through the ensuing years that I hung onto those words... "just 'cause I love her."

Love had not been a dominant factor in my life before I met Jerry. My mother held me only once that I can remember. When she came toward me I usually flinched because I thought she was going to hit me. Usually I was right. If I had a scowl on my face, she slapped me. When I asked her what I had done to deserve that, she would coldly reply, "I don't like the way you look." Although by many standards mine was a terrible childhood, I made up my mind early on that Mama's actions would not determine my destiny. I would live as positively as possible.

Looking back on those formative years, I think of how fortunate I am to have survived and to have had so much more than I ever dreamed possible. Just the living room in one of our homes was larger than three of the houses I lived in as a child in Wyoming.

During my pre-teen years, I realized that anything was better than my forgettable childhood. Mama and Papa were Italian immigrants. At age fourteen, in Italy, Mama had worked for rich people who often beat her and slapped her around. Being beaten was all she really knew.

Although my parents had been processed through Ellis Island, they would never share their stories with us. Their lives were hidden within themselves. My brother and I were like unwanted onlookers. One of the few things I do remember Mama saying was that she had accepted Papa's proposal of marriage only because it meant she could come to America. Going to America meant escaping her circumstances.

Since my father was a coalminer, we lived in a coal-mining town. There was no love in our house.

Mama told me I had been delivered by a midwife. She said I had weighed ten pounds and my body was covered with black hair. To top it all off, my head was badly shaped. She was so embarrassed by the way I looked that she felt she had delivered a monster. The constant reminder of that description left a scar on my heart.

Early on, I was taught to scrub floors, and to scrub them again if they didn't meet the standards of perfection Mama had. We owned no carpeting—everything was linoleum—and my job was to keep it spotless. I shed many tears while on my knees with a brush and a bucket.

My fingers were constantly slapped if I held a crochet hook incorrectly while I was learning to crochet. More hatred followed and provoked more tears if I made a mistake when crocheting or if I didn't concentrate enough to suit Mama or measure up to her standards of what little girls were supposed to accomplish.

While I was a child, my best playmate was a little baby lamb I had pleaded to be able to keep when the flock left it behind. It meant I would have something to love that would love me back. The lamb followed me everywhere and was a friend. Then came the dreadful day that I saw it hanging upside down, with a poker through its head and its blood dripping onto the ground. I cried for days and could not forgive my father for having killed my lamb. Now I realize that we may have needed it for food, but nothing of the kind was ever explained to me.

Papa beat Mama often, until one day I saw her pick up a butcher knife and throw it at him as he ran away. It stuck in the door jamb.

Papa left.

Mama was on her own.

I recall several incidents in the years that followed that left their mark on me. One of them was the time I was chained to the porch because I forgot where I had put some money. Then there were constant embarrassments in front of my friends. At times I prayed to God to let me disappear into thin air, then later said thanks for those unanswered prayers.

My brother and I were often boarded in places similar to today's foster homes. The first was in St. Charles, Michigan. I have wonderful memories of our time there.

The lady of the house baked bread and pies, and we had animals to care for, and, more importantly, a family atmosphere. We did chores like pulling weeds and helping with the crops. Although the fields appeared hundreds of miles long, good food awaited us when we got home.

We gathered eggs of every size, and then, when we were served eggs for breakfast, we tried to guess where they had been gathered. In the spring we picked strawberries and were glad to do it. To this day I keep strawberries in my yard to remind me of those happy times.

Once, in the middle of the night, we were awakened and bundled up to go out and witness the birth of a calf. Being very ignorant of such an extraordinary event, I was frightened by the afterbirth. Earlier, when the cow had been bred, we smaller children were told to go into the house. Of course, we did not, but instead hid in the barn and watched the proceedings. As the bull mounted the cow, we really didn't know what was going on, only that it seemed a strange exercise.

We rode horses bareback. There was no television or radio. We walked two and a half miles each way to a one-room, red schoolhouse, swinging our lunch pails. Luckily the roads were cleared in the winter before we made our way back to school, warmly tucked in our snow gear. The snow appeared sky-high.

At school, we each had a special hook where we could hang our coats. Even having a hook to call my own was thrilling.

In the summer we took shortcuts through the woods. We were allowed to be children, but were nonetheless outside the special bonding of the birth-children in the household. Still it was an adventure.

After our stay there, Papa moved us closer to where he had taken a different job. It was another boarding facility, and we cried at having to go. I remember hanging on for dear life to the apron strings of my surrogate mother, then being harshly pulled away by my father. This time we were put in a smaller house with a foster mother called Jenny, who had two children and whom I grew to love.

Then a dark day dawned. We were driven to the local courthouse and taken into the judge's chambers. My mother was contesting our living with Jenny although we were happy there. When we arrived at the court, my brother and I ran to Papa, trying to understand what was happening. We had to sit very still as we heard all the reasons why he and Mama should have permanent custody. There was a lot of yelling. I was scared to death.

The judge finally announced his decision: I was to be awarded to Mama; my brother would go with Papa. This was our first separation. Not seeing my father was bad enough, but to be apart from my brother was excruciating.

Mama took me to Detroit, and I cried all the way. She tried to console me, but I was brokenhearted.

Detroit was such a big city, with houses built close together and more cars than I had ever seen. The noise of the streetcars and the neighborhood assaulted my senses.

On the sticky, hot days of summer, the city would sometimes cordon off a half-block or so and open a fire hydrant. What a way to cool off! Since there was no air conditioning in our modest area, the surging water offered much fun and relief for the kids. This was my first taste of what it would be like to have a swimming pool.

My new stepfather, Mike, was quite nice to me. In fact, that year was the first time I remember having a Christmas tree. On Christmas morning I hugged and kissed Mike for all he had done, because I knew the effort had been all his. I never remember Mama putting herself out for anyone.

That holiday season was a magical one for me. Although I did not get the skates or bicycle I had dreamed of, I did get my first doll.

In later years, I learned that Mama had insisted that girls did not need such foolishness, but should be taught instead how to do women's chores. (By the age of fourteen, I could have run a household, because she constantly reminded me that all I had to worry about was keeping house for a man.)

When Mother became pregnant I was left out of all the activities—like the baby showers—and preparations for the coming child. But finally, the day of the birth came. I was sent to stay with the neighbors downstairs. No one bothered to tell me what was going on. I remember seeing the doctor's car pull up in front and watching as he hurried up the stairs carrying his ominous-looking black bag.

The bedroom I slept in that night was directly beneath Mama's. Mama was in so much pain that I heard her screams throughout the night. The more she screamed, the more I cried. Finally, there was quiet. The next morning I saw my beautiful sister, Anna May. I was so happy to see Mama with her big belly gone and not screaming any more.

Unfortunately, that was also the day I was enrolled in Mama's school of raising and caring for babies. I was ten at the time, and for the next three years I always seemed to be carrying Anna May. Mama and Mike worked at the Chrysler plant, and since their hours varied, I was the built-in baby sitter with a lot of responsibility.

My stepfather's relatives lived in Pennsylvania, so we drove there to visit them once or twice a year. One winter we got stuck in a snowdrift while I was asleep in the back seat, and when I rolled over and hit the door handle, the door flew open and dumped me, face down, in the snow. Had the car been moving, I could have been killed. By the grace of God I was not. He had another plan for me.

On one of those trips to Pennsylvania at Christmastime, Anna May became very sick. My step-grandfather worked for a company with medical insurance, so he called the company doctor who came to see her, gave her two aspirin, and left. She grew steadily worse. Her nails began falling off, her ears were draining, and her complexion was paper-white. Mama finally called another doctor, who diagnosed her as having scarlet fever. He gave us little hope of her survival.

Because I had been the one who took care of her the most, Anna May would eat only for me. She was so weak. I held her and read to her by the hour. Five days after the diagnosis, the doctor started an IV, but by then it was too late. We took turns watching as her tiny, fragile body slowly slipped away from us. She died at the age of five.

She was brought home in a small, generic, white casket and placed in a corner of the living room. The casket was kept closed because of the fear of the disease spreading. I was sad, frightened, and scared, and avoided the living room. I felt as empty as her little bed was. Like the baby lamb, but much more dear to me, another beloved playmate was gone.

On the day of her burial, I was left at the house alone. When the family returned, all the joy my sister had brought to our house left, and the holiday spirit was shattered. Before returning home from Pennsylvania, we placed a wreath on the front door. To this day, a wreath is a symbol of lingering grief for me.

Life in our home when I was growing up never resembled "The Waltons" or "The Ozzie and Harriet Show." It takes time to strip back the layers of the past and to realize that all those involved in my early years probably did the best they could. It is easy to see raw, ragged faults and to be impatient and hurt by them, but the years have helped me lose the irritation, discouragement, and exasperation I experienced. It was a long time before I could take human failure off the hook, but the day I did, I was at peace with God, Mama, and that newly understood child within my being.

Chapter 2

Although no one will doubt a star was born on March 16, 1926, in Newark, New Jersey, early life was not a barrel of laughs for little Joseph Levitch, also known as Jerry Lewis.

Jerry's folks were part-time entertainers and because of this, he was left alone a lot. His first feelings of belonging came from his much-loved grandmother, Sarah Rothberg. (His times with Grandma were the basis for portions of his film, *The Delicate Delinquent.*) She had a way of giving him security and the love he needed desperately.

When Danny Lewis, his dad, called Jerry to the stage in the President Hotel in Swan Lake, New York, and coaxed him to sing, the applause and the crowd's other reactions obviously filled at least one area of need Jerry had and put back together a few of his life's broken pieces. At five years old, he was getting his start.

He later related to an interviewer that it was not until he was eight that he performed again, and was quick to add, "And there wasn't such a thing as unemployment insurance."

Jerry was a lonely little kid who wanted to grow up to be a clown—and he did! Jerry never failed to be good for a rapid deployment of laughs—no matter what the circumstances or at whose expense.

When called on to perform, Jerry did. He possessed the capability and capacity to make you laugh—often until you cried.

People who study the roots of comedy are quick to say that much laughter comes from tragedy. And many agree that Jewish comics are often superior to Gentile comics. The reasons are legion and make sense to me: They rarely come from upper-class neighborhoods; they are used to expressing themselves clearly and quickly; they are familiar with street-level life and possess *chutzpah*—a generationally imparted street wisdom that emerges from put-downs, isolation, prejudice, and the fight for acceptance and survival.

Steve Allen wrote an appropriate description about the little clown who grew up to net millions of laughs— and dollars.

When Jerry Lewis is funny, he is so exceptionally funny that you have to go on a sort of vacation to get over it. He's not subtle or warm or gentle or sophisticated or fey. He's down your throat, in your ears, buzzing in your brain. The jokes come so fast, the seltzer bottle squirts so often, the pratfalls are so hilarious that once ever so often is enough.[1]

Steve is right. I have always been convinced that Jerry's body language has become like a minutely refined and fluently spoken second language. His antics and contortions set him apart from others in the field—a vast field of those who survive and those who fall out of the spotlight—broken, forgotten, and victims of an usually destructive career.

Mel Brooks said of Jerry, "[He] was an exciting, dynamic creature and I learned a lot from him. But high-key comics like that always burn themselves out."

That kind of comedy burnout was evident quite often in our lives. Once was when ABC-TV signed him to "The Jerry Lewis Show." I was both excited and nervous because there was talk that I might try my hand at the commercials. The staff encouraged me, but I felt somewhat timid at the prospect.

As we prepared for the show, there were lots of meetings and rehearsals. Opinions ran rampant on what Jerry was expected to do on this hopefully long-running show. Being host to a late-night talk show had provided its share of casualties, but Jerry was ready. Ready to do it all himself and feeling adequate. He signed a forty-week contract. The year was 1963.

At last the stage was set! The lights went out, and the show premiered at the Hollywood Palace Theater, (later renamed Merv Griffin's Theater) which was located close to Hollywood and Vine—the prestigious address of show biz for so many glitter-filled years.

The children and I sat in a box specially designed and constructed for us. Since Jerry always carried a picture of us for good luck, the producers put us right on location—visible, vulnerable, and—in my opinion—valueless to the show.

It aired for a very short span—less than fourteen weeks. NBC was accused of making a bad decision to take a comedian who, at best, does a short show with lots of distance between appearances, and attempting to transform him into a personality who would appeal to late-night audiences. There were many hurtful consequences.

Steve Allen, someone I have long admired, was quick to do a take-off of that opening night scenario. I am not sure if it injured Jerry or me more. Steve's parody, set on his own show just a short time later, was a recreation of our new show. Cameras, action, even the boys and me in the box were imitated—surrounded by guards appearing to be more like Wild West gunmen than either our personal bodyguards or ABC's security department employees. In my opinion, it was satire at its worst. But I am sure a lot of people laughed even as we cried.

In the past, the boys and I had been the brunt of Jerry's jokes on many occasions, and we had survived. We would live through this, too. Again, I was reminded that one person's tragedy is another's comedy. Who could hold it against Steve? I couldn't.

Another time of trial for Jerry was when he was touted as the new sensation for the musical *Hellzapoppin*. Musicals were a somewhat unfamiliar genre for him, but he was to bring to this one the wit and zaniness that had been a hallmark of the 1938 Ole Olsen/Chic Johnson freewheeling review.

The show's pre-forties presentation had the crowds literally in the aisles with laughter. Could Jerry put this script in his mouth and play out the actions of insanity? The producers knew he could, and I think he did, too. His cool, clunky grace and individual panache had proved adequate before. Jerry has a well within himself from which he draws all sorts of needed solutions. I have seen him draw on that reservoir, successfully, many times in my life.

But the final consensus on the show was that it was doomed to failure. This time, no pails full of wit emerged to keep it from the canceled column, even though it was re-edited for a shortened season on television.

Reviews rarely bothered Jerry outwardly. Inside, who knows? He often liked to quote Sam Goldwyn's adage: "Don't pay attention to the critics; don't even ignore them."

Jerry would then say, "As an individual, it makes me happy when they approve of what I do. On the other hand, as a member of an audience, if the critics tell me I shouldn't like something that I've liked, I resent it, and I like it even more."

However, critics said Jerry's stage debut produced nothing the audiences had not seen before. Others were kinder and felt the leaks that had led to a sinking ship could be plugged. They were not.

There are still those who remember *Hellzapoppin* and say there were lots of laughs and who can judge Jule Styne and Company's music? But for Jerry, it turned out to be the first four letters of the title—HELL! And when he suffered, we suffered, too. Jerry, the one who could give audiences long moments of magical Lewis-style silence and get away with it, withered when any show or performance was silenced.

In discouraging and down times, Jerry became very demanding. When the demands were not met, he got frustrated and spent the night in his bathroom. I often wondered if his wanting sandwiches or attention in the middle of the night or in the raw, early dawn hours were the ways he tested to see how much I loved him. I sometimes felt my emotional reactions were childish; his, too.

He perceived his bathroom—which was equipped with

a telephone, television, refrigerator and other amenities that seemed to calm him—as a haven. I asked for and was granted—for a short time—an extension of the bathroom phone line by our bed. But he soon cut the line and had another, different number installed in the bathroom, and I had to endure overhearing his conversations with other women, and then conceal my frustration and hurt. I still haven't determined if I mentally and emotionally repressed those times to protect myself or the children.

One of the saddest quotations in all literature is Thoreau's, "The mass of men lead lives of quiet desperation." It was so true in our lives. I think both of us were devoid of the precious and motivating commodity called self-worth. At any rate, I tried to fix things. Over and over again. I'm not sure about Jerry.

Although close associates know Jerry has never tried to be what he originally was, he still has difficulty being what he has become. Richard Gehman, a biographer, stated: "A human being becomes a performer because he does not like what he is, or does not want to face it, or wants to hide it from others. His survival depends upon living this lie. He cannot bear to think that others may realize it is a lie. He must be 'The Image' at all cost."

The cost is high for a star who believes his own publicity.

I have read the backgrounds and histories of a lot of people in comedy. So many share backgrounds similar to Jerry's, and I feel deeply for them all. My life, too, was very much a parallel to theirs, and that's why I have such a soft spot for these performers. I have also encouraged my children to stay away from the "laff-making business."

The opposite was true of Jerry's folks. Both his mom and dad made friends with the Browns, who ran a resort hotel in Lakewood in the Pine Woods section of New Jersey. Danny and Rae Lewis told the hotel proprietors about Jerry's producing, directing, and acting in his own little show at school. He might have been twelve at the time. The Browns were elated. In time the family moved to work with the Browns, and Jerry became a bellhop, busboy, and hotel entertainer. In his early teens, he entertained into the night and coped with school as best as he could during the day. School was his comedy of earned errors. The skinny, awkward boy was dubbed, "teacher's regret." This term was not surprising since Jerry attended thirty schools in two years of touring or being deposited temporarily at someone's residence.

Jerry's dad performed for years—in those burlesque days—with Robert Alda, Alan Alda's father. Various accounts say that Jerry overshadowed his dad's performances and that led to jealousy on the part of the elder Lewis. Whatever the reason, Jerry moved on. His dual roles at the hotel, as well as stints as a shipping clerk, soda jerk, and so on ad infinitum were embryos for future roles which helped lift him beyond himself and those unhappy, unkind circumstances that sabotaged the nurturing he needed.

Jerry started doing his own creative impressions— entertaining "shorts"—on the Loew Theater circuit. From what he used to tell me, he was good, and the people loved him. It was a tough way to make $15–20 a night, but his irrepressible spirit kept him moving ahead— inevitably, though not instantaneously—toward stardom.

I will always admire Jerry for his loyalty to his parents and to mine, even in the rough times and in spite of their controlling natures.

As our children came along we occasionally talked to Jerry's folks, who had moved to Florida after his dad retired. When his father suffered a heart attack, Jerry tried to find ways and make schedule changes in order to visit. For a time he brought his folks to California, paying for their stay in a hotel until an apartment could be found for them. Even though I visited them quite often, I was never a substitute for the son they wanted to see. Nor were our children.

When Jerry's folks came to our home, they showed little affection for the boys, who were given a quick, impersonal kiss before being relegated to the background.

Not a profile of the grandparents I had hoped for. But all of us had a background of co-dependence and family dysfunction. (I am convinced that in those areas the past has no future. We do the best we can and move on, seeking to do better. I like to think the present is given in order that we may act with a view to the future, and make it better for those we meet.)

Jerry's parents are buried in Nevada, and with them, hopefully, some of Jerry's pain about his early life. One can never be sure. The public may think that when Jerry does his acts and performs in a physical manner, his face gives a clue to what he is thinking or feeling. But Jerry has an inventive imagination. He can be what he wants to be—and only he knows what that may be.

A well-worn story illustrates my point. Remember the druggist who had a lifelong dream of taking just one vacation to Florida? One day a genie popped out of an apothecary jar in his pharmacy and promised to take care of the store while he was away on his long-desired vacation. Shortly after the druggist left, a customer came in and sat at the counter of the soda fountain. He said to the genie, "Make me a strawberry malted." So the genie pointed his finger at the customer and said, "All right, you're a strawberry malted." In just such a manner it seems, if Jerry wants to write, he *becomes* a writer. If he wants to direct, he *becomes* the director. If he wants to be the star, that's who he is. If he wants to turn everyone's life upside down, he becomes a human tornado. He has the propensity to will himself in so many constructive—as well as destructive—ways.

Like the proverbial wanderer, destined to lead a touch-and-go life, Jerry feels he can go anywhere he wants to and he'll be there.

[1] Steve Allen, *More Funny People* (Briarcliffe Manor, N.Y.: Scarborough House)

Chapter 3

Life was a little different for me, although it too, was filled with pain, even in the midst of what joy I experienced. An event from my adolescence is typical.

There I was, poised on the brink of my future! With my little band, I was playing for a Polish wedding—the Nyzinskis'—in Hamtramack, Michigan. We were exhilarated because this was a paying performance.

The wedding party led the dances. Everyone was brightly dressed in colorful costumes or apparel from Poland. Hamtramack was a community of dear people, who held tightly to the ties of their homeland.

We had started at one o'clock in the afternoon. (We were the star performers according to the Nyzinskis. Of course, we were the *only* performers!) We finished at two the next morning, and were handed our money—$15 each. Our group, Esther and Her Sailing Swing Band, was headed for good things. We headed home in separate directions, clutching the payment that was the realization of all the previous months' practice.

Tired but still euphoric, I opened the door to our house. Mama met me in a rage, hurling all sorts of accusations at me. I tried to interrupt the flow of her tirade to explain we had been working, and to ask if she had forgotten about the Nyzinskis' wedding.

I gave her the money, thinking this would calm her down, since money was always scarce at our house. Instead, as she started hitting me, she screamed that I had gotten the money from having sex with boys. I ran from her and huddled in a corner of our tiny kitchen.

She kept coming. When I curled up enough to make it hard for her to reach me with her fists, she began kicking me furiously.

I will never understand her outbursts. I do know each one left me with a choice: to succumb to the verbal and physical abuse, or to try to overcome it. One of the ways to do this was through music. Music brought me joy as nothing else did, so I started to learn everything I could about instruments and reading music. My voice was slowly developing. Somehow, I had to go beyond the depressing, confining limitations Mama strictly enforced. During those later teen years I came to recognize that I possessed the power to choose what would happen to Esther Calonico—even the power, shortly thereafter, to change my name to Patti Palmer, which was a drastic step in our Italian household.

(My name had always been a source of frustration for me. Mother called me "Little Pasqualina," which means "Little Easter." It would have been devastating to me to attend school with a name like that! Mother relented at that point, agreeing that I should be called Esther. It was as close to Easter as she could get. Patti later became my legal name.)

The power to choose also meant making a decision to be either upbeat or downbeat, optimistic or pessimistic. Where did the choice between being upbeat and being downbeat come from? The downbeat attitude was nourished by Mama and the teacher who led the "singing vocal class." When we first auditioned, this teacher listened disdainfully to my performance. Singing in front of the class was hard enough, but enduring her piercing look, which could have penetrated steel, was almost unbearable. When I was only a few measures into my song, she stopped me abruptly, "Your voice is only good for barrooms," she said. I was eliminated from consideration for any solo parts.

Because I was short, I was placed in the front row of the choral group. We were not separated according to the part we sang, but were placed only by height, so that the teacher might achieve her ideal, uniform look. Just before our first performance, she instructed us to wear long evening dresses. Mama refused to give me the money, so I went out to do another performance with my band. The $17 I earned purchased what I thought was a nice dress. Even though it was second-hand, I was delighted to have something to wear. When the teacher saw me, her negative attitude climbed up on stilts! I was relegated to the back row, completely hidden from view, unable to see anything or be seen.

(I still wonder if that dress really belonged on Mr. Blackwell's list or if there were other, hidden reasons for her actions.)

I never remember a word of affirmation from that teacher. Never an encouraging remark or a suggestion to keep on trying. Although the group sang well, we were just another class to be tolerated until the semester ended. None of my friends had any kind feelings for her either.

In contrast to her negativity, a very gifted music teacher, Mr. Alvey, was an optimist, and the sweetest man I had ever known. He loved life. He cared for his students. We felt important around him. We were treated as individuals, not as a mass of humanity. He made us laugh and pushed us to the limits of whatever talent we possessed. It was wonderful.

One day in the school corridor, he noticed that I had been crying and took me in his office to find out why. Gently, caringly, he coaxed my concern into the open— Mama had not come home the previous night. By now it was just Mama and me living in an upstairs apartment, and I had no idea where she was. Was she dead? Alive? Ill? Kidnapped? My imagination ran wild.

Mr. Alvey asked me if Mama had a boyfriend. When I replied affirmatively, he suggested that she might be with her friend and simply could not make it back home. But he didn't stop there. With fatherly concern and carefully chosen words, he told me the facts of life in a way I had never heard them before.

At some point between entering and leaving his office

that day, I started growing into maturity. I'll always be grateful for him—a teacher who encouraged me to be the best, and yet warned me about the real world. I have always wanted to express my thanks to him, not just for his verbal instruction, but for putting the thought inside my head that I could be a star.

My accordion teacher was another upbeat person. He let me know I was good at music. I learned fast, and perhaps I should be grateful that Mama made me practice, practice, practice. Yet the practice, combined with more sewing, embroidery, cleaning chores, and her constant obsession with scrubbing, left little time for me to enjoy sports.

I always won when playing marbles, though. It made me proud to know I was so good that the boys teamed up with me. The same was true in baseball. I had a natural swing. (Maybe that carried over to swing music a few years later!) But I was a mitt-less catcher, because mitts were not in our budget, and one day I grabbed a missed fastball and painfully bent my finger. That injury kept me out of play for many months—out of playing baseball, the accordion, and even scrubbing. I look back to that time as my very first vacation.

For years, Mama and my stepfather had me play at the Chrysler picnics as well as for their friends. When I was a very little girl, my stepfather would lift me up on the bar in a smoke-filled tavern, and have me perform for his acquaintances. Oh, how I hated the smell of alcohol! Being given my first silver dollar is my only good memory from that bar.

Then, during a labor dispute when Chrysler was on strike, Mama thought it would be a good idea for me to go over after the lunch hour and play a little soothing music. One day, I brushed against John L. Lewis, the famed union boss.

My musical education continued. With the accordion now mastered, I moved on to the trombone. Stretching my short arms, I became second trombonist, then graduated to first-chair trombone. That was another joyful day, even though there continued to be no encouragement or praise from home.

I progressed to the xylophone and then to the drums, which I wanted to learn because I had a real crush on the drummer. I learned the bass fiddle because the violins and cellos were all taken. I carried that huge instrument on my hip at school every day. (Good training for later carting around six boys on that same hip!) I learned nearly every instrument in the band and developed the ability to transpose to any key by sight.

With each new opportunity, I pushed myself to the limits of being positive about life.

There was real anticipation the day the accordion teacher found a small slot in which I could perform at a local radio station. I really felt I had hitched that accordion to a star—a tiny, unknown, low-power radio station.

On the few occasions that the accordion teacher had made passes at me, I had responded with disdain and had been able to brush them off. But the day we completed our trip to the station, it was different. I had done a good job. The station was pleased and had told me so. Celebration was in the air. As we got in the car, the teacher reached for me, kissing and pulling me toward him. My anger must have frightened him because he made me swear never to tell my mother. This time, though, the lessons came to an abrupt end, and the incident left me with a mixed image of men.

However, graduating from high school was like graduating to freedom, even though my graduation day was sad. No one came to see me receive my diploma, and there was no money for prom activities. After the ceremony, I used fifty cents I had scrounged from beneath the sofa cushion to treat myself to a movie. It cost twenty cents for the streetcar, twenty cents for admission to the theater, five cents for a Holloway sucker which lasted all through the show, and I walked home with a nickel still in my pocket.

After that, I took a job in a little music store, Grinells, and loved it. At the store's entrance was a baby grand

piano where a pianist played show tunes and popular
songs all day. I learned them all, and hummed as I sorted
and ordered music, and cataloged. I also joined an all-girl
band, still dreaming about becoming a star. The all-girl
group became a freshly discovered galaxy to me.

With the band, I sang, and played accordion and
trombone. I learned Tommy Dorsey's theme song. People
enjoyed it, although they must have laughed as I sang
with a big, red ring around my mouth from playing my
trombone. With two instruments and my voice, I was
called a "triple threat (or treat??)!"

During those days, things moved rather swiftly. My
music counselor arranged for me to have a full music
scholarship in Florida. This would have been a great
opportunity to learn more music theory and broaden my
education, but Mother flatly refused. No way would she
allow me to go to Florida. She said all I would do is play
around and get married. She was right. I would have
played around—with a lot of instruments! Unfortunately,
her decisions were final, never debatable.

Instead of going to Florida, I was hired, for tips, as a
strolling accordion player/singer in a nice restaurant-bar.
On breaks, I listened to the jukebox playing Dinah Shore
songs. I quickly learned those and picked up her style.
From there I got a job as a staff singer at NBC in Detroit.
I sang with the house band for a time, then, as I improved,
they offered me my own program.

"Two Pianos and Patti" went on the air as a fifteen-
minute segment. We rehearsed and planned to make it
upbeat and fun. The radio station staff were good to me.
I did a lot of the music I had mastered from the
background sounds of my music-store job and from the
jukebox in the restaurant-bar. Dinah Shore songs have
always been my favorites. In fact, songs became the friends
I had rarely had when I was growing up.

From doing "Two Pianos and Patti," I became known
to a lot of servicemen, and was asked to do USO shows.
Entertaining the men in the military was a privilege. They
were teases, but they loved to dance. At ten cents a dance,

all the dance girls did well—but the musicians did better. While I was singing on one of those radio shows, Ted FioRito heard me on his car radio and called the station to find out how he could contact me.

In those days, Ted FioRito, who had written the popular, "Toot, Toot, Tootsie, Goodbye" was well-known as a star-maker. While some referred to his music as rinky-dink or trite, people followed him and his shows were always packed. He was the band leader who had brought Betty Grable and June Havor to Hollywood. At the time, they were part of his band, and they did little "shorts" for movies. That's how they came to be seen by talent scouts and introduced to the movie moguls, after which they both became box-office stars.

I will never forget meeting Ted at the Cadillac Hotel and being asked to join his band. He hired me on the spot! It meant I had to leave the two pianos behind, because Patti was moving forward. It was a red-letter day, and the beginning of a special association.

For once, Mama did not have a lot to say. (Little did she realize I would be getting married, anyway—although not in Florida.)

Ted taught me a great deal. About how to walk on stage, how to hold a microphone, and how to dress. I stayed with his band for a year and did we travel! We performed one-nighters in lots of army and navy bases and continued doing radio shows. We played the Roseland Ballroom many times. (I never ceased to be impressed by the beauty of women in classic formal dresses and men in tuxedos.)

The band was made up of top-notch musicians. Later some left and joined other greats. One night Louie Belsen, the drummer who married Pearl Bailey, came by and asked if he could sit in for a couple of numbers. Ted said yes, and Louie was thrilled, as was the band. Being a lover of drums, I could have listened to his artistry all night. Those drums talked, rolled, and beat as I'd never heard them before. Sometimes I wonder if my son Gary got his love of drums and bands from his mother. Big bands will always be a part of me.

I thought I had really arrived the day Ted asked me to introduce one of the songs he had just written, working off his original lead sheets. That day I felt accepted for the first time. There were other times later, but that was the sweetest.

I was part of a group called the Swingles. Ward Swingle—who today enjoys a respected career with his group of baroque singers in Paris—did all the arrangements for us, and they were great. He was my real teacher of harmony. He was a master of blend and balance. What a priceless education I obtained... with pay!

The night before I met Jerry, we had played a one-nighter a few hours away from Detroit. Ted and his manager had flown on ahead. The band, singers, and instruments were loaded into a truck with benches lining both sides, and a small, two-foot board at the back. I won't forget that mode of transportation. It was a hot, August night. The air felt good, but we were packed in like animals. We had worked so hard the night before, and were leaning on each other trying to get some sleep.

Suddenly, we heard the roar of a truck coming up behind us. Unfortunately, we were without taillights. Everyone screamed to our driver to move over. He pulled off the road, and we jumped clear in the seconds that followed. The driver of the on-coming truck had not even seen us. It was another of God's miracles that we were not hit from behind. The driver sped on by, unaware of the close call. We were shaken for a long time.

Although it was very late when we got to the hotel that night, we still had to be at rehearsal on time. So, the next morning, wearily, and still a little in shock from our near-disaster the previous night, I headed for the theater. That was when I met Jerry Lewis.

Ted was not pleased with my instant infatuation with Jerry, and our dating caused a lot of tension. One day when I was late for a rehearsal, Ted said, "I suppose you were out with that Jew again." It was too much for me. I gave my notice. After my final performance, all the Jewish musicians left with me. It had a crippling effect on Ted's band. I was sorry for that, and sad that he held such harsh feelings toward a young comic who needed a break.

Before I left FioRito, I had been called by the Jimmy Dorsey staff. Jimmy was looking for a singer, and they wondered if I might be interested. They asked me to send a picture and some air checks. After the scene with FioRito, I sent my resumé, hoping another position would be offered so I would not have to face unemployment or consider going back to Mama. Much to my delight, I was hired!

My first engagement was at a theater in Pittsburgh. I had never even rehearsed with the Jimmy Dorsey band, and was replacing a stunning professional. I remember standing in the wings and listening to Jimmy's magnificent arrangements and the unique sounds of his fabulous band. Then Dorsey came over and said I would be doing the next show. I was petrified.

The arrangements were in a key lower than my voice, and were also more intricate than the ones I had done with FioRito. I found myself straining just to touch the low notes. When I finished, the applause sounded as if it came from a trio of people. What a disenchanting feeling in a very crowded room! I knew I was not any good at all. As I left the stage, the other singer was ranting and raving, demanding that her name be removed from the marquee. She didn't want anyone to think it was her singing.

But things improved—a lot! The arrangements were adjusted for my voice and working became a joy. Seeing "Patti Palmer" on the marquee was a delight. It also made me work harder, vocalize more, and strive constantly to improve. Soon, Henny Youngman joined our group as the "comedian with a violin."

We went on to the Capitol Theater on Broadway in New York, where we worked with the movie, *Thirty Seconds Over Tokyo*. We were backup for Pegleg Bates, that wonderful, black dancer. Those were the days when the band rose up via elevator, and suddenly appeared in the audience's view. It was always a thrill to see them materialize from nowhere. The crowd would cheer and the place would become electric as the band leader joined them.

Jerry often sat in the audience and watched us perform. One night I sang "A Tree Grows In Brooklyn," which always brought a good house response. Jerry seemed proud and maybe a little prejudiced in my favor as I sang with Ted Walter (who later died of a drug overdose).

Schedules in those days were killers, but we were forced to keep pace or move on. After doing five shows at the Capitol Theater one day, the whole band went to the recording studio after the last performance of the evening. It was not like it is today, where you tape the track and then the singer sings to it. Teddy and I were doing a duo in the style of Helen O'Connell and Bob Eberly. Adjusting to recording was rough, especially when I was so weary from our grueling schedule. By now, I was also pregnant, and at four in the morning, people were uptight. We still had rehearsals and five performances to do the next day.

On top of it all, it was my birthday. What a day!

Another memorable event occurred when we were working the Capitol. After the show we were to go to the Apollo to take part in a charity event. While I was standing in the wings, Joe Louis, the boxer, came along with some of his army friends. We all watched Ella Fitzgerald sing onstage with Chick Webb and his orchestra. Chick was doing drums and the people exploded in applause. Then came Patti Palmer, in person!

(How does anyone follow a legend like Ella? We met years later and she remembered the occasion. What a star!)

During one show at a Pennsylvania hotel, Tommy Dorsey came by, wanting to play in his brother's band. He was pathetically under the influence of alcohol, but someone loaned him a trombone and he started to play. It was awful. It seemed to me I had played better when I was with my own band years before.

At the Adams Theater in New Jersey on a New Year's Eve, one of the acts prior to ours was an acrobatic one. That night the three acrobats balanced chairs, leaving one of them to sit in the top one. Jimmy, full of liquid spirits, insisted on climbing to the top chair. Everyone waited, almost in suspended animation. We needed our jobs and our leader. To our relief, he made it. It was an amazing feat!

I was a dedicated fan of the music of Glenn Miller, Artie Shaw, and Benny Goodman. To perform under their guidance and musicianship was the dream of all good singers.

I had made my first public appearance in my high-school auditorium playing the accordion and singing Miller's "Moonlight Serenade." To this day, I adore that score. It brings such warm memories of a unique time in America's music.

When Miller was overseas in the Air Force with his band, I received a call from a good friend who did arrangements for Miller and FioRito, wanting me to audition. I mailed him an air check and sent Miller's agency a picture. I was ecstatic to think that the great Glenn Miller wanted to hire *me*. There was one obstacle, however—I would have to join the military. It was a tough decision, but I really felt I couldn't go overseas. I wonder if I had made a different decision, whether I might have been on the fatal flight which took the lives of Glenn and so many others.

Glenn Miller used to say, "You don't have to be a star to be in my show." Those close to him agreed. You were already a star just by having received the invitation to work with him.

Sometimes I think Glenn's words were applicable to the Lewis family. Jerry was the star, but because of him, the family was placed under the hot lights of public scrutiny. I know many people dream of spotlights and will do everything in their power to move toward them, but I am also aware that the system that makes you a star can send you into oblivion if there are no backup lights.

I have been in many kinds of light and darkness. I've endured the darkness of the bar in which my stepdad showed off his little daughter to crass drunks. I've been in the back row of a "singing vocal class," hidden from sight but nevertheless performing with all my ability, on pitch, glad to be part of a group. I have had my own band and sung with good ones. I've done picnics, the USO, and Polish weddings, and have been invited to join the great Glenn Miller. I have performed on radio and television and seen my name on the marquee.

Jerry has headlined all over the world, and for years, I was a star in his life. But as I look back, my most comfortable place has been in the wings, not under the lights. I like the role of being a support to anyone who needs me—not my voice or instruments or perceived status, but just me. I have learned that the greatest gift I can give myself is to give myself away to others.

It took me a while to come to the beautiful conclusion that no one has to be a star to be in God's show. All he asks us to do is walk in His light, reflect his goodness, and help others move toward the light.

That is something I can do on or off the stage, in my home with my family, or through my church.

Best of all His rewards endure.

They that be wise shall shine as the brightness of the firmament and those who help others, as the stars forever and ever.

—Daniel 12:3

A long-time friend, Gilda Maiken Anderson, a musician herself, and I have kept in touch sporadically through the years. She is kind in her thoughts about the past:

I knew Patti as Esther Calonico on Uncle Nick's Kiddies Hour on radio station WJKB in Detroit. The show aired five days a week from 3:30 to 4:00 p.m., and we performed on separate days. It was a very popular show for youngsters aged five to fifteen years.

Patti was beautiful, an accomplished, natural musician. Our acquaintance began at Cass Technical High School, a prestigious, highly-rated school that gave opportunity to people at all economic levels. The school's music department has been a model throughout the United States for half a century. Their graduates have gone on to great careers in jazz, big bands, classical, opera and symphonic orchestras.

Patti was involved in everything musical in that school. I watched her play the marimba one day and skillfully perform on the drums the next. Her voice was professional without coaching. She played easily. Her long, gorgeous hair fell down her back and was the envy of a lot of girls. She had a quiet personality.

We both inched into professional careers during high school, Patti to bands and I to Johnny Desmond's quartet.

No one doubted that Patti was headed for an impressive career. She had a lot of cheerleaders on the side. Although her career changed to wife and mother, she was the strength behind Jerry. I once heard someone say that Jerry had the face that launched ten thousand pies. Patti's gentle face kept life sane at home, and helped launch Jerry and her six "little men."

Chapter 4

Jerry's tiny *Instruction Book for Being A Person* contains these recommendations: Help people, Help a friend, Have a friend, Be a friend, Keep that friend.

I believe the last three points symbolized his deep desire for friendship with Dean Martin and heightened his hurt when he was unable to *keep* Dean as a friend.

In many ways Dean was Jerry's idol. Jerry studied Dean's charm, looks, appeal to women, and general demeanor. Dean was nine years Jerry's senior, and benefited from those maturing years my husband had not yet experienced.

When they were a team, Martin and Lewis were touted on billboards as "the hardest act in show business to follow." After their breakup, which was as painful as a divorce, I recall telling Jerry the hardest act he would ever follow was *himself,* and I think that was prophetic.

There are many interpretations of the era of Dino Crocetti and Joseph Levitch—or Martin and Lewis. Their meeting, ten years together, and subsequent breakup are still discussed and debated. Many sources of information about that time were unreliable or lacked hard evidence. Dean said very little about the demise and Jerry's hurt prevented his discussion of it. Writers contrived piecemeal stories, born of agents, friends, club owners, and tidbits—many edited to the point of inaccuracy—from publicists.

My recollections are simple and uncomplicated. My journals help validate what went on during that magic, frustrating, storybook, and hugely successful decade. Most likely, parts are incomplete because I was relegated to the role of mother, not news collector or commentator.

Jerry had known Dean only in passing before the eventful day that started their career as a duo. They had worked together briefly at The Glass Hat in New York, and Jerry was convinced that Dean had talent. Although they had barely said hello when their schedules crossed, Dean remained in Jerry's mind as they toured the nightclub circuit.

When our son Gary was two weeks old, we planned a night out in New York while Jerry was working the Havanna Madrid, solo. I was delighted to sit in on his show, and watch his great pantomime and lip-sync routine. A huge poster in the foyer of the club announced Dean Martin as a coming attraction.

At the end of the act, we went to Lindy's for cheesecake. Dean was nearby at an "A" table with an assorted group of his cronies. Recognizing Jerry, he invited us to join his party. We were delighted. This was my introduction to the man who would become an integral part of my marriage to Jerry, or perhaps more accurately, my marriage to Martin and Lewis.

There were lots of jokes and much kibitzing going on at that table in this celebrated restaurant. Dean was in charge, but Jerry played it well. I understood afterward what Jerry meant when he said, "Dean is a worldly man... just too much!" It was an exhilarating ending to a perfect evening, one of the few in which I had been included up to that time.

Not long after this, Jerry was working the 500 Club in Atlantic City. A male singer in the show, with rumored connections to the Mafia, was so awfully flat and terrible that the management was in a panic for a fast, last-minute replacement. Enter Jerry! He was quick to suggest that he knew a singer, and that the two of them would be great together. In fact, he suggested they could be a comedy team.

Dean agreed to accept and Jerry was elated. At last he would have a partner, and best of all he would fulfill his desire to work with Dean.

Their first show did not go as anticipated. They were supposed to be a comedy team, but Dean just sang and Jerry was the comic. There was no feeling of being together, no *esprit de corps*—only two guys doing solo acts onstage together. Then the ever-present light bulb in Jerry's head went on with 1,000-watt illumination!

After showing Dean how to hold a mike loosely and waiting for him to start to sing, Jerry started clowning. Suddenly the chemistry poured out like a cinched-up hose releasing a gush of water. It was a start—a giant start toward an unbelievable future. They perfected their routine. With Dean singing, taking the mike off the stand, and Jerry doing his crazy antics, both tapped a well of talent neither had previously used. They just did what came naturally—being a goof and a goof's partner.

Because of Jerry's pixie, juvenile qualities, people did not get too upset with his foolishness. In fact, some women in the crowd wanted to mother him, while others focused on the handsome straight man who was sometimes likened to Rudolph Valentino.

Jerry was forever writing new schemes and twists for their routine and studying the results, and it was not long before they took the world by storm. In those days, Martin and Lewis could do no wrong. Their salaries soared; agents and audiences jammed the rooms. That was in 1946.

After a show at the Copacabana, Jerry was beside himself with joy, saying he wished he could have been in the audience during the performance—it was so good he longed to see it himself. That kind of confidence carried the two a long way. Obviously, the box office and gate confirmed Jerry's confidence.

During the next ten years it was non-stop success. We moved from our little apartment to Hollywood, renting a home in Beverly Hills.

I flew to New York to be with Jerry while he and Dean were doing six or seven shows a day at the Paramount Theater. I was thrilled to be with him, but not six hours after our reunion, I had a call from home saying that Ron had fallen and had a spiral fracture in his leg. The pediatrician thought it best for me to return. I left that evening on one of the old prop planes for the nine-and-a-half-hour flight back to mothering.

On other occasions I did catch the shows. Dean and Jerry were so good. Dean was the straight man and Jerry, himself—the lovable fool, the comic, the clown, the child I loved so much—bringing to every performance a chapter from his life. (I have concluded that much of Jerry's performance was a catharsis for his own emotional difficulties.)

In the late forties, whatever they did made them the talk and the toast of the town—any town—they visited. And on into the fifties, their position as number-one act was rarely disputed.

The contrast between the two men didn't change as they matured. The stunts and songs changed, but they were still Dean, 100 percent gentleman, and Jerry, 100-proof joker. Some kind of a combination.

Then came films. First, *My Friend Irma*, followed by a sequel. I think Jerry was best in the sixteen films he and Dean made together. I tend to agree with the observations of some who study movie production that Jerry was better at being directed than at directing himself. (One insightful writer suggested that when Jerry was in the director's chair, there was no one left to veto him. He liked having the final word and usually demanded it.)

Jerry used to tell me that every person is really two people. He certainly was—the husband and father who was solicitous one day and vindictive the next. The husband who, on many occasions during this time, decided not to come home at all. It had happened when Gary was a baby and we were in New Jersey, and it contrasted drastically with the husband who said his main source of strength was Patti, not Dean.

Dean and Jerry were playing the Capitol in New York when Jerry announced our second separation. His parents were elated, for now they would have their son all to themselves. They lingered backstage and milked the parent role for all it was worth. I was hurt, not "playing" hurt. I loved Jerry and our little ones deeply.

During this particular estrangement, his folks worked hard to undermine my place. Their attitude—Our son is finally back!—should not have surprised me. I had never been the little Jewish mama with real Jewish roots. To them I was Patti the interloper, the Italian outsider.

My awareness that Jerry was not faithful was gradually growing. A friend confided that Jerry had had our family doctor fly to Florida to discuss some of his problems and answer questions about the ramifications of someday leaving me. (The same doctor was called to Hawaii on another occasion for a similar consultation.)

In retrospect, calling in a physician from thousands of miles away rather than an attorney or advisor appears to be a deviation from the norm. But then, one rarely encounters normalcy in the middle of a nightmare.

Even though the doctor may not have been a counselor, he did give Jerry advice several times, and maybe it was helpful. In my heart, I will always believe Jerry came back to me because I provided some stability in the home and with the boys. I was grateful when things worked out, but too immature to see a developing pattern. My vows to Jerry had been "forever" vows—the kind that are not broken, so I did not understand his view of marriage.

Dean's first wife, Betty, the mother of their four children, was an interesting woman and a casual friend. When I learned that Dean had started bringing a new heartthrob to the second show after Betty's departure, it caused me some concern. But Jerry kept reminding me that Dean's personal business was not ours. Because of my background, and because I always felt like an underdog, I really hurt for Betty.

During this span of time, Jerry occasionally spoke about moving away from Dean. I always agreed to whatever he wanted. Their differences were becoming more troublesome and visible. Jerry was also astute enough to know the "alimony" they would have to pay—in films to be made, appearances scheduled, and the like—would

affect them both. By now they had appeared with Ed
Sullivan, Bob Hope, and on "The Texaco Hour," and
working out the settlements would require a team of
lawyers. The big question was, were their differences
irreconcilable?

Part of the problem stemmed from their differing
personalities. Jerry was forever giving away their services
to charities. An avid reader, he tried to make up for lost
school time. With his sharp mind he studied comedy
and cherished everything he could find on his idol, Charlie
Chaplin. He liked the Chaplin quote: "Through humor,
we see in what seems rational, the irrational; in what
seems important, the unimportant. It also heightens our
sense of survival and preserves our sanity." We all needed
our sanity preserved as Jerry incessantly suggested routines,
wrote scripts, and planned. I never doubted that he was
happiest when he was working. (The joke told about Jerry
was that he worked so long and hard that when he opened
the refrigerator and the light came on, he would do fifteen
minutes of comedy before making a sandwich.)

Dean was the antithesis of this. He was laid-back and
he headed for the golf course whenever possible. Although
a lot of people said he drank way too much, I never saw
him seriously inebriated. (The joke told about Dean was
that he drank so much his liver ran for cover when he
lifted a glass.)

Obviously, these two would always have a future, but
would it be anything like their past? Both had an
entourage of staff and hangers-on. Jerry surrounded
himself with those who would laugh in the right places
and rubber-stamp his decisions, just as I often did. Dean
was his own man—most of the time.

Jerry had what he called his "Creed Book" in which he
noted all sorts of sayings and goals. He once scribbled
"Humor—a marvelous instrument. If used properly it can
suffocate a lot of ugliness out of people."

The goal that failed to materialize during my time
with Jerry was his desire to be on Broadway. The scuttling
of *Hellzapoppin* thwarted that dream. However, plans call

for him to perform in another Broadway show, so perhaps he will be able to cross that goal off his list, too. Jerry was a firm advocate of the belief that the harder you work, the luckier you get.

I think that if Dean had a creed book it had more to do with relaxation and living for the moment than revving up for another day. Was he lazy, or laid-back? Opinions vary. I believe he liked working just enough to keep him living in the style to which he was accustomed.

During those days of uncertainty about what the future held for us, I seldom looked back. Rather, I was a shock absorber, attempting to reduce stress and create a buffer for Jerry's creativity. Fragments of memory cross my mind and pierce my heart as I think of those years when Dean was woven into the very fabric of our lives, and then of the time those tangled threads started to fray.

I have memories of the four of us—Betty, Dean, Jerry, and me—eating at Leon and Eddy's, a popular New York nightclub. Betty, who showed no ill effects from drinking, advised me to try sparkling burgundy. After a couple of drinks I became so ill that I rarely drank again. That night I told her about the first time we had joined Dean's table at Lindy's and we laughed nervously at the recollection of thinking the weekly $125 salary was the most we could hope for.

There are memories of nights when Jerry and Dean, playing the Copacabana, finished the second show and joined us, all dressed in our finest jewels and furs, for a tour of Harlem to listen to the jazz greats of that era.

While Jerry and Dean were playing the "Copa," Dolly Sinatra, Frank's mother, went to see them. She thought there was a strong resemblance between Frank and Jerry, and often referred to Jerry as her second son. Sometimes, feeling devilish, Jerry would comb his hair like "Ol' Blue Eyes" and stroll along Broadway, causing people to chase him, thinking it was Frank.

In 1953 in London, Dean and Jerry performed at the military bases in the daytime and played the Palladium in the evening. Despite the fact that they were incredible—

the British press termed them a "smash"—there were hecklers that night, and toward the end of one of the shows, one of them incensed Jerry. As we started to leave the theater, the hecklers were waiting. Jerry went after them, but was restrained by Albert Broccoli (the producer of the James Bond movies). It was my first experience with that kind of situation and also my unfortunate introduction to an unkind American press. Stateside, a huge story about the incident emerged and mentioned only the fracas while totally ignoring the magnificent performance of Martin and Lewis and their reception by the British public as a whole.

In the latter years of the partnership, there were times when Jerry was being impossible and I, in my role as a buffer, would receive a look from Dean which said, "I know what you're going through, but I can't do anything about it." Others in the group were also aware of his behavior.

No one is perfect, but keeping harmony so that Jerry and Dean could make the world laugh was like trying to hold mercury—any harmony that existed was fragile and illusive. But when I ·watch what they used to do, I am reminded again of their enormous talent and am grateful that I was there to see it firsthand.

Some years ago I went to a benefit at which Dean performed. He looked older and so tired that I cried all the way home. By contrast, Jerry still appears vital and performs frequently. When I see either of them on camera, they seem to be enjoying the moment, but I still see and feel the insecurity of the past.

I think the following descriptions of Dean and Jerry— then and now—are pretty accurate.

Jerry is a great comedian, a child star, even though well into his sixties. He's often depressed, inconsistent, ever in motion, charming, talented, imperious, tyrannical, has a high-anxiety level, is energetic, extroverted, self-destructive, creative, a party-hater and do-gooder. His perceived teacher was Charlie Chaplin.

Dean is a study in slow motion, is suave, a good

communicator, unsure, a ladies' man, charming, talented, a ladies' man, laid-back, slow-paced, introverted, a ladies' man, creative, a crooner with great looks, a golfer, party boy, and ladies' man. His perceived teacher was Bing Crosby.

Frequently during our marriage, Jerry was very jealous of any other man's attention to me. He even accused me of having an affair with Dean. I did not. We were like family. But the verbal abuse Jerry heaped on me sometimes had me on my knees, crying for mercy. (Now I am convinced that his accusations and tirades were a cover for his own activities.) Over the years, I had heard the stories but refused to believe them for a long time. Dean tried, in his own way, to offer me support, and just knowing someone else was aware of what was going on eased my pain. It also created a bond between us and helped me understand Dean's feelings about what would soon transpire—the end of their partnership.

Each time Jerry discussed the potential dissolution of the partnership, it was apparent that his heart was on the line. I think that, in delaying the end, Jerry was actively wishing the problems away. I honestly believe he knew for a long time the breakup was inevitable, since both he and Dean were tugging in opposite directions on the anchor that kept them together.

Jerry never told me what the actual straw that broke the back of the team was. I do know he had accepted, without consulting Dean, a charity gig. Jerry went, hat in hand, apologizing and asking Dean to do it. Dean said he would, but didn't show up. That night may have been the final oversight—real or planned—on Dean's part.

The last film the duo made together was *Hollywood or Bust*. And "bust" they did—permanently! For Jerry, his film title, "The Day the Clown Cried," was descriptive.

Their final appearance as a team took place at the Copacabana on July 25, 1956—precisely ten years to the day after they had started their landmark journey to the top.

Many fans thought the "last appearance"

announcement was a gag, like many others they had pulled off. The press wrote copy about who would trigger the "makeup after the breakup." But it was no gag. Dean and Jerry were the highest-paid act in show business, but money does not buy personal miracles.

That last act was only partially routine. They walked onto the stage amid a great fanfare of lights and applause, and they performed full throttle. The last song was "Pardners" from one of their Paramount movies. The crowd shouted appreciation and hurled words of encouragement to keep them together: "Don't separate!" "You're the best!" "Hurry back."

But there was no turning back. It was over. Once seen as closer than brothers, the two now became strangers.

Jerry called me from the dressing room. I could tell his moods by the way he addressed me; as Esther—my given name—when we were in the past; as Patti, when he was angry with me; as Momma when he needed consolation. This night it was Momma.

I reassured him, saying that everything would be fine. It always was. Jerry would make it on his own. Then I started to make plans for a trip to divert his attention.

Dean shook hands with his partner for the last time in a surprise appearance in the pre-dawn hours of the "morning after." His arrival in that tension- and pain-filled room was almost medicinal. Dean did what all of Jerry's staff and well-wishers—Joe DiMaggio, Sammy Davis, Jr., Leo Durocher, Polly Bergen, Nanette Fabray, and others—had not been able to accomplish. Their comments were not the painkiller Jerry needed. He was looking for the broken-off piece of the act, and the emotion of the final handshake was shrouded by the knowledge that they might never be back together again.

I watched Jerry rise to his potential in several incidents that followed. Few people are aware he has a good voice, not just the quirky squeak he uses for imitations. He is highly intelligent, and it was that intelligence that made him aware for a long time that this split had been inevitable.

What Jerry lacked in empathy for his family, he felt for others. He was aware that his inner, sensitive emotions were telling him that Dean was sick and tired of being number two when the team was number one. And Jerry knew he had imposed most of his desires on their act. Even though he kept reminding Dean, "You are the spark. You are talented," I don't think Dean was listening, or else he was just tired of Jerry making most of the decisions. Jerry used to say, "If I were the straight man, I'd resent the comic too, 'cuz he gets all the press and attention."

What was little known about the show was that Jerry wrote, produced, and directed many of their routines, though it's difficult to find that on any script. Jerry just did it. Dean just took it—but only for so long. Would the split destroy them? Never. The only one who could destroy Martin and Lewis was Martin—or Lewis.

It was not until 1976, during a telethon, that they appeared together again. That meeting was staged by Frank Sinatra and lasted only a fleeting moment. A hoped-for renewal of past friendship never occurred. Jerry used to say, "I'm still waiting."

Gilda Maiken Anderson toured with Jerry and Dean as a member of the Skylarks, and had this to say about the last tour before the duo split:

Our group, the Skylarks, had finished performing with Harry James, the last of the big bands, and were looking for another opportunity. It came through Nick Castle, a choreographer and producer who had worked with Dean and Jerry. We first appeared with them on the "Colgate Comedy Hour" in New York. It was a great experience.

I observed Jerry during these years, knowing he was married to my friend, Patti. He was generous and kind to all of the performers. He talked about Patti and was more than protective of her.

On our last tour with the duo, we had performed an enormously successful two-week engagement at the Copacabana. We completed a variety show, "Judge for Yourself," with Fred Allen, then embarked on the last segment of the tour—eight weeks of theater stops, taking a train designed to be both transportation and accommodation.

One railroad car was for Dean and his entourage, another for Jerry and his buddies. The third car was designated for the musicians, the Skylarks, the Stepp Brothers, and a few others.

Dean spent a lot of his time playing cards; Jerry was vitally full of energy and rarely stopped entertaining. Even after long performances, he would board his car, then, like a kid, come into ours to do his "gig" again.

The trains hooked onto major lines from city to city—a plan which, to date, I understand has not been duplicated. On the whole trip, we never saw any anger or disagreement between Dean and Jerry, nor caught any whiff of discontent.

I can't explain the climate in the first rehearsal after we arrived in Los Angeles. We were at Ciro's, rehearsing for Dean and Jerry's show. All hell broke loose when the word of the breakup spread.

Supposedly, each would continue on his own. The backups were dumbfounded, stunned, and rocked. There were hardly any adjectives to describe our feelings and no explanations that suited us. The headlines blared the ending, but no one had logical, sensible answers as to why. The situation remains a puzzle to us all. We know the symptoms, but have few theories on what caused the root to wither on such a productive vine.

The Skylarks finished out our commitment without the two headliners. Ciro's brought in huge stars to attempt to fill the gap—people like Tony Martin, Peggy Lee, George and Gracie Allen.

One of the lasting memorials to Martin and Lewis is a street named after them in Atlantic City. It remains today. The rest of history we know—or coyly surmise we do; we go on holding individual thoughts about what might have happened.

The years have gone by. Both Jerry and Dean have continued to work. Jerry's success in film kept him financially secure for a long time. Dean stayed busy in various roles and at clubs. Some still speculate that Dean might have been richer had they stayed together. Richer, Martin admirers admit, but miserable. Again the public was made aware that the wild, frantic years were *still* over.

We took a trip after the breakup of the duo, and outwardly, Jerry appeared to relax. On the trip, a series of unexpected events caused me to realize again that somebody up there was watching over us.

We were in Las Vegas. Judy Garland was appearing at one of the hotels and we decided to catch her act. Little did we know when we made that decision that Jerry would be the show!

During the afternoon Jerry was asked by Sid Luft, Judy's husband, to be her replacement that evening. She was losing her voice and simply was not going to be able to go on. Accompanied by Jerry's publicist, Jack Keller, we all went over to the hotel. As we approached Judy's suite, we could hear her crying. When she insisted on seeing Jerry alone, Jack and I went downstairs to squander the $300 in chips given to us by the hotel management. As I kept winning, I came to the conclusion that one only wins with other people's money—a premise I continue to hold.

After a while, Jerry reluctantly announced he would do the show—his first solo since the breakup. I kept offering encouragement to counter his admitted feelings of inadequacy. Then he came up with the idea of asking Judy to sit on the stage while he performed. That way the audience could see her and know she really was unable to sing.

I was seated with Harry Cohn—head of Columbia at the time—Sid Luft, and some others. Then it happened. Jerry started singing Judy's "Rockabye My Baby" and continued with other Jolson songs. At a golden moment, Judy arose, and with her raspy, sore, deep-throated voice, singing above her laryngitis, she joined Jerry. Together they were belting out music! The crowd went crazy. Harry was in tears watching how hard she was trying. I thought both of them were real troupers. It was another time when Jerry did what he did best... which was whatever came into his head.

As we went out after the show, I felt a wifely smugness, knowing that Jerry had done it again. I think I realized then that the "kid" was growing up and, as Jack Keller remarked, doing it by recognizing that he was still the kid, and that wasn't so bad!

The sound of "Rockabye My Baby" was the introduction to another verse in our lives. Jerry started recording with Decca Records. The sales of "Rockabye" topped four million, and his career was off and running once more.

During those years, Jerry spent money like an impoverished kid who had hit a bottomless jackpot that included unlimited tickets to Disneyland or Any-land. The disruptive strain of his personality emerged at home, where he remained more director than husband and father. We carried on that way for many years. I feared his temper and was not assertive enough to do battle. I just kept trying to hold everything together.

Don't misunderstand me. There were many wonderful and special events, both with and without the children. Some have never left the good-memory section of my mind.

One such memory was dining with the legendary Sophie Tucker, who definitely had a mind of her own! She was not hesitant in being critical in an effort to be helpful. At least I am sure that was her intent when she came onstage after a Martin and Lewis performance. People cheered as Jerry introduced her. But, taking no bow, she immediately ripped into Jerry and Dean for their antic demolition of the stage. She thought they were the greatest but did not like it when they tore off clothes, cut ties, threw things at each other and played the part of juvenile wrecking crew. Sophie made her point! She was great. She called Dean and Jerry "a mix between the Marx brothers, the Keystone Kops, and Abbott and Costello."

Through my ups and downs, Sophie remained very dear to me, and her friendship is like a trophy standing on the shelf of my heart, long after she is gone.

I think, even after so many years, that Dean may be a trophy loosely held in Jerry's heart. Just where he will ultimately be placed, I do not know, but I am certain that he will have a place.

Chapter 5

A publicist once noted, "There are exactly *seven things* that dwarf the Lewis dedication to the performing arts. They are Patti, Gary, Ron, Scott, Chris, Anthony, and Baby Joe. They make it all seem worthwhile."

That particular publicity piece about Jerry's talent and dedication to the family made me happy. Still, I wondered how many realized that I also lived with—seven things—seven boys, to be precise, the eldest being that irrepressible comedian the publicist had lauded—Jerry. The one who was convinced on numerous occasions that he was just an insecure nobody in a world full of somebodies. The one who cultivated those insecurities amid spasms of lucidity.

With six small boys and one large one, life was quite a challenge for me.

Throughout their childhood and adolescence, our six kids struggled for their identity while desperately seeking their father's approval. Each was tender, innocent and very vulnerable.

I have often thought that Jerry enjoyed the children much more when they were younger than when they were approaching adulthood. He loved to see their reactions when he jumped, fully dressed, into the pool, or catapulted a hunk of food to the ceiling in our formal dining room. (This was forbidden behavior for the kids, but funny when Dad did it.) They depended on him for fun and games... especially a game of baseball. But as they grew, the process of their developing minds of their own was difficult for Jerry to handle. I guess it's hard for a "child" star to cope with grown-up problems.

When we had a crisis, or if I were ill, Jerry coped by distancing himself from the problem. He simply ignored any unpleasantness, but later would sometimes try to atone by bringing gifts. Nevertheless, while he grew in the ways of comedy, I grew into assuming more and more responsibility for the family.

Jerry's energy, drive, and obsession about *giving* away so much of his time and talent frequently collided with his lack of awareness of things that were happening in the world outside. As a rule, he was detached from meaningful relationships outside show business. I know from his letters, magazine comments, and scattered moments of seriousness how hard he struggled to define his role with the family and with me.

My formula was to love my family and receive their love in return. I knew I had to teach the children the same kind of love so they would emerge happy kids—the opposite of what Jerry and I had been in our youth. Now, I realize, our marriage contained precious few role models of genuine love. We had received no training in the give and take a marriage requires. We possessed no understanding of what stardom does to Hollywood families, and we had only had glimpses of the value of abiding faith. Perhaps that's why all eight of us have experienced our uncertainties and times of difficult discovery. I pray hard that the future brings the blessings of peace and joy to all. I sincerely believe it will happen. "For faith is the substance of things hoped for, the evidence of things still not seen." (Hebrews 11:1)

I kept a clipping from a *Herald-Examiner* from more than twenty years ago. It was one of those "behind-the-scenes" type of articles that brought up again the *seven to one* odds. The headline read:

Behind the Scenes with the Lewises

HE RAISES $5 MILLION

SHE REARS SIX SONS

There was a slight mistake in the headline, for I was truly raising seven.

After I became pregnant with Gary and married Jerry, we struggled financially, since I was no longer working and Jerry's gigs were scattered. But it was a simpler time of sharing and joy. A time when diapers were made of cloth, when you made your own baby food, when going out to dinner was a major luxury, and when a dollar bought more than a meal. Our apartment, like Gary, was tiny. And how I loved both of my "boys."

Mothering came naturally. It was wonderful, although caring for a new baby was a real learning experience (even though I had helped with my half-sister). I always tried to treat the children the way I wished I had been nurtured.

Helping Gary, and later, his siblings, develop a sense of security was not easy when Jerry was away so much. So I usually remained with the children when Jerry was on the road. How can children develop self-concept and security without the presence of at least one parent at home? That may be an old-fashioned point of view, but it's what I believe.

I had never felt a personal sense of belonging until I became a musician, and even though the feeling was sporadic, it helped me. So I felt it was important that Gary know he *belonged* to us; that we were family—bonded forever—no matter what happened to any of us.

I am proud of what Gary has done with his life, venturing out on the uneasy road to success with his band and turning negatives into positives. Gary has mixed memories, but agreed to share some of the good ones.

Gary: *I remember my dad always giving me bits and pieces of information intended to help me through life. I think he knew we were all spoiled, so he was trying to help us prepare for life outside the "mansion." This quote from his 'Creed Book' stayed with me. "Treat people on your way up in life the way you want them to treat you, in case you come down, 'cause you'll see them all again."*

The thing we did most together was play baseball or go to Dodger games. Dad always took my friends and me to ballgames, and even bought the empty lot next to our house and turned it into a baseball diamond for us. He even played with us at times. He had shirts made up with team names and bought enough equipment to completely outfit two whole teams.

We also traveled. The first trip that I recall was in 1953, when we sailed to London on the Queen Elizabeth I when Dad and Dean were doing a show at the Palladium. After a train trip in France we celebrated my eighth birthday in Cannes. The French Riviera was so much fun: swimming in the Mediterranean Sea and eating rum cake were highlights. We all laughed when Mom gave the kitchen staff a good scolding for serving children cake containing rum.

I also enjoyed seeing Dad in the movies and realizing that all those people were laughing at my dad.

Ron, our adopted son, was a special gift from God. I was as excited about bringing him home as I was about the five I gave birth to. Ron was such a gorgeous child.

Gary and Ron attended Black Foxe Military School. They both participated in the regular Friday parades: Gary played clarinet in the band and Ron, a very small boy at that time, was present with a wooden rifle on his shoulder. He reminded me of a little toy soldier in a Christmas window.

One particular Friday, Jimmy and Gloria Stewart, whose two sons were also students, arrived, accompanied by General Omar Bradley. I treasure my picture of six-year-old Ron—dressed in full regalia—standing there in all his innocence, saluting General Bradley—also in full regalia.

Ron was known for goofing up when he was younger. He wanted so much to please his father, that as soon as Jerry uttered, "Go get... " Ron was out of the door before the sentence was finished. He would then have to return and find out what he was supposed to get. At times we laughed about it and at times it upset Jerry very, very much. (Those times passed.)

Ron is reserved with his memories. Some are hurtful, I know, like those of all of the boys. But he is talented and has made his way. Ron went on the road, telling some of his dad's stories. The time he spent with Jerry working for the Muscular Dystrophy Association has been vital for Ron. I believe he learned a lot from those experiences. He has always had a good heart.

He confided to a friend that as he sat in church last Father's Day and listened to the sermon on fathers and God the Father, it brought to mind the last time he had seen his dad. On that occasion, Jerry had not even acknowledged his presence.

Ron grew up with mixed messages: With Jerry the celebrity, things were nice and quite sensitive. With Jerry at home at dinner, the celebrity disappeared to be replaced by an angry, controlling father.

Ronnie says he has learned the hard way to appreciate his own family, trying not to imitate his father, whose response to anything that went wrong was to say, "I'll fix it." He meant to, I hoped he would, and sometimes he did. But often the relationship stayed broken, or the dilemma went unresolved.

Ron found consolation in isolation in the thirty-one-room place that was our home during his maturing years. Yet even during the times he distanced himself, he still managed to pick up most of Jerry's mannerisms, and, almost unconsciously, his body language.

One time Jerry sent Ron to a 4-H convention in Columbus, Ohio. He had written Ron's speech, which was directed to people in America's heartland, had taught him the antics that should accompany it, and had scripted everything. But when Ronnie started, it was terrible. Even though he had memorized the jokes, they were second-hand, and the audience knew it. So he put the script down and started doing it his own way, in his own words. By the close of the presentation, three thousand kids were on their feet.

Ronnie recognized a fact of life that day. Trying to recite your father's words doesn't mean you can be your dad. Even though he still uses some of Jerry's words, he is now 100 percent Ron, and is very effective doing seminars for corporations.

Ron said recently, "If there is anything to learn from the past it is that there was a lot of pain in my life. I grew up in the fairy-tale fifties. Pain was standard. We did not handle it well because there was some hidden, implied rule that, if you were the offspring of a famous parent, the pain should remain concealed and things would work out. We don't live by hindsight, but it does pull us forward to make better choices and realize we are responsible for our actions. Blame is never a functional response."

Ronnie has learned boundaries by observing. He is negotiating conflict. He has attempted to put what he calls the "fairy tales I lived in" behind him.

Being a forever mother, I wish that, like the Wizard of Oz, I could take the children's bad memories away. However, that old Wizard was really more of a coach than a wizard, making those he confronted use what they had inside. And Ron has used what he has inside. So I'll stay on the sidelines and keep rooting for him and the others.

There were many years between Gary and Ron and Scott, who came along at a special time. Scott's heart often outpaced his body. The older boys enjoyed him both as a "pest" and a "pretty neat little kid."

Scott is my sensitive son, simple, yet complex, like his dad; tender and compassionate. He was one of the boys who grew up eating caviar (which all the children loved) at Chasen's, where we celebrated many occasions. David Chasen was Scott's unofficial godfather. We hosted Jerry's mother and father's 50th anniversary party there, and Chasen's did a lot of catering at our house.

Scott was a youngster you wanted to hug. His infectious smile caught your heart. But he was also the one who needed a bridge of hope built over his everyday skirmishes. Scotty wanted things right and liked happy endings. (If only young mothers could foresee what was ahead and understand how much their children need preparation for the tough journey to adulthood, it would help those children immeasurably.)

Recently, Scott shared his happy and sad recollections.

Scott: *I always felt that my dad was there for me. I remember, growing up, how taken for granted Dad's presence was... even when he wasn't there. (We knew we could always reach my dad by phone. He always told my brothers and me that.) So even if he was halfway around the world, we knew if we needed him, his presence could be felt to help us. Either he'd just talk to me in a comforting way or he'd offer a solution to my problem. Growing up, that was a wonderful way for my father and me to bond.*

I felt my dad always treated me in a friendlier, or more familiar, manner than my other brothers. He never opened up to me as if we were friends, but he always told me I was special. Special because I was "his first son as a man." (My dad was thirty when I was born.) He'd also call me a "miracle baby" because I was conceived after my mom had the operation to enable her to have more children. I was also the only one of the children he never hit.

I loved sitting next to my dad on the couch in our living room, as we watched the footage he had shot the day before. With his lighted clipboard in hand he'd make notes on everything that needed work and explain to me why he was doing what he was.

I learned a great sense of perfection in this business from my dad. When he was happiest—at the studio—Dad was extremely productive and definitely brilliant. I still marvel at some of his works.

I remember the evening my dad came home after John F. Kennedy was shot. I had never seen him look so sullen. He wasn't himself. As a child of seven, it was hard for me to conceive what that event meant to my country, but I think my dad was in shock at seeing someone even more powerful and influential than he, and a good friend besides, having his life snuffed out. My dad became extra cautious after that.

I have loving memories of my twelve years in Catholic school. Everything I am today started there through our Lord. I really realize how much I owe my teachers and my mom. In high school I bonded with my history teacher—Brother John Dobrogowski, who was Polish—and we're still in touch. He was a film and sports enthusiast who instantly recognized my interest and appreciation for film.

My dad spoke at my graduation ceremony in 1974. He was funny and inspiring, and everyone enjoyed his speech. When I came up to accept my diploma, my dad got up out of his chair, grabbed me, and kissed me on the lips (which is where we still kiss).

We always "did" Christmas day as a family. Dad always had the camera rolling to record our reactions to the presents we opened. He would yell at us when we wouldn't face the camera, and then my mom would yell at my dad that it was Christmas. We always had breakfast together in the dining room on Christmas morning. It was the only morning of the year that happened. (We usually ate in our portion of the house while Mom and Dad either got a tray upstairs or ate in the dining room alone.)

Travel with Dad was usually going to San Diego to go out on the boat. Mom took us on a lot of great trips and was always very attentive. We went to Vancouver, Canada, once and had a terrific time. (Dad would never have stayed at a TraveLodge.) Mom always let us be involved.

I don't recall an actual time of awareness of seeing my dad in movies, on TV, and in print. But I've always loved his movies. He made me laugh on screen and in real life. I admired his work then and still do.

We really did stay in a TraveLodge on that trip to Vancouver. The kids loved the city and its old-world atmosphere.

I treasure one of Scott's letters to his brother, Gary, when Gary was en route to Korea in 1966. Scott seemed older than his ten years.

Jerry often said how proud he was that I was such a good mother. He was encouraging, yet at the same time, I felt his jealousy of the time and love I lavished on the boys. He was not predisposed to share me that much, and I had trouble knowing when to draw the line. At times, Jerry seemed unreasonable, but now I understand

DEAR GARY,
 I HOPE YOU ARE ALRIGHT.
I HOPE THEY ARE KEEPING
YOU WELL. WE ARE ALL
PRAYING YOU WONT GO TO
VIET NAM WHERE YOUR
LIFE COULD BE WAISTED!
BUT IF YOU MUST DIE FOR
A GOOD RESONE, YOU WILL
DO IT FOR YOUR COUNTRY.
BUT IF YOU DIE BY THE
KNIFE OF AN ENEMY SOLDIER
YOU WILL GO TO HEAVEN
AND BE AWAY FROM IT ALL
BUT LETS PRAY THAT THIS
DOESNT HAPPEN, BUT LETS
PRAY YOU GET SICK (NOT BAD)
AND WILL SEND YOU BACK
TO US. LET THE LORDS
BLESSING BE WITH YOU,

          YOUR EVERLOWING
             BROTHER,

        SCOTTY

PS. WE ALL LOVE YOU

it a little better. As one of my "boys," he needed a portion of child love along with adult love. So, in an attempt to resolve the conflict, we had another child.

Chris, our fourth son, is a go-getter and very motivated. When he was five or six, he watched me put on some culottes, then commented, "You look like you should be playing 'crochet'" Of course, we laughed at his pronunciation of croquet.

Life has not been smooth for Chris, but he has faced with maturity situations beyond his years. In our home, the things he accomplished rarely merited acceptance or acknowledgment by Jerry. Chris was an "A" student in oceanography, ecology, and art, but his ratings in English, religion, and history slid off the far side of the scale in the opposite direction, causing Jerry to call him "stupid." That hurt me as well. But Chris was good at weighing actions and understanding the underlying motives. He has been able to work with his dad in the marketplace, on the telethon, and in production capacities.

His thoughts on the past helped me bring into focus some of the troubling events that transpired in our home. He reminded me that all the children were aware of more during our difficult years than I gave them credit for.

Chris: *I thought my dad was the greatest man in the world. I thought that because I was always seeing people wanting to be with him, it made me really special when I was with him. I also thought he was a very loving and generous father, because my mom was always telling us how much he loved us and that everything we received was from him as well as her.*

I remember telling Anthony once that our father really loved us a lot. I knew this because I always heard him say it on television. I also remember feeling very special because when he came home, Dad always made us feel loved and important, even if it was only for a few minutes. It meant a lot to us.

I was also very scared of him when he became angry. (Mom was usually on the receiving end of his abuse.) He yelled so loudly that we often wished he would hit us instead of yelling. We most definitely would have deserved it if he had.

I always thought Dad was the funniest man in the world, and I always smiled when he looked at me (I do even to this day). I can remember not being able to eat on many nights at the dinner table because he was making us laugh so much. I was always excited to see my father.

I felt Mom was always there to protect us when Dad got angry, even if it wasn't with us. She always cushioned the fireworks. It felt good knowing there was always someone on your side, no matter what you had done.

As I matured I knew that my parents weren't very happy together. I had the dubious honor of sharing the door between my father's bathroom and mine. Through this, I could hear my father speaking on his bathroom telephone with other women, then talking on the intercom with Mom in other parts of the house, or just muttering to himself.

It was not uncommon for me to hear Dad talking to Mom in his dressing room, then walking into the bathroom, locking the door and calling a girlfriend to say he loved her. This shocked me at first, but by the time I was about eighteen, I had heard enough to have a pretty good handle on just where my mom was coming from. This gave me a better ability to understand her short temper and sometimes hurtful attitudes toward me because I knew what she was going through. I loved them both as much as ever—and equally—but it was hard trying to understand why Dad was never around anymore.

Despite this, my childhood home was a happy place. My home now is similar in many ways to the one I grew up in. I think all of my brothers and I feel extremely nostalgic when we talk about our home together. It was a wonderfully warm, happy environment that was always a treat to come home to. I have tried to pattern the environment around my children after the best of what I had—and never to do what hurt me.

My kids, Josh, Tatiana (Tia) and Morgan, are told many times a day that they are loved. There is a lot of hugging and kissing and positive reinforcement throughout every day. I sing them the bedtime songs my mom sang to me and I make the Italian Christmas cookies she used to make every holiday season.

The element most similar to my childhood would have to be the tsunami of love that hits my kids every day of their lives. The most important difference would have to be that I never ignore the feelings of any of my children. When I enter the door and Tia comes running to me with her arms lifted up, I pick her up, and kiss her, but, in contrast to what my father would have done, I turn instantly to Josh and his smiling face and embrace him with the same amount of love. I will never let my problems or daily hassles make my children feel as if they aren't the most important things in my life, because they are. I don't think Dad was neglectful when he came home, but what he didn't understand was that if you only come home once a month, your children have built up such a level of anticipation for the moment that when the door opens, they need to feel as important as the event has become to them. (This was not the case every time, but happened frequently enough for me to remember the feelings.)

Even though we loved our nannies, we tormented them. Anthony, Scotty, and I turned torture into a delicate art that walked the tightrope between childish pranks and disrespect. We knew that if we looked innocent enough, no matter what we did it would not be reported. If we crossed the line to disrespect, we knew that my father was only a phone call away with "the belt." This was considered certain death. As I recall, only Anthony ever got "the belt," but Scotty and I watched. It was very educational.

I think we all imitated Dad doing funny things as we grew up. We did pratfalls, made loud, silly noises, made faces, and did regular comedy in school routines. I wanted to imitate him as a photographer (I became a famous one). I wanted to direct and produce films (I have), and I wanted to help needy people (I still do). But in all of this I was doomed to disappointment when I tried to show him what I had become.

It was not until later in my life that I understood the fact that my father's insecurity was the basis for his outgoing nature and was used to cover his fear of not being accepted or loved. So when I tried to make him proud of me, he had no idea how to accept as a compliment the fact that I wanted to be like him. My desire to emulate him did not come from what he had done for me or given me, but because I recognized his true inner talent and goodness. To this day, because of his own insecurity, he can't acknowledge the fact that any of his sons may be as good as he is at something. When I finally figured that out I was able to accept it and have a great relationship with him, which I have to this day. I still want to be like him—but I won't tell him that!

In 1978 I made an animated film—my first—for Dad, but it was not received very well. I've worked as a pro-celebrity tennis tournament coordinator and have made a film for the government. When I started writing pilots for Paramount Pictures in 1980, it was like coming home.

It was also in that year that my parents split up, and my relationship with Dad was very strained for the next couple of years, until I heard he had been taken to the hospital with heart problems. After his surgery, we became much closer. He became a person to me for the first time ever. His illness was a real turning point in our relationship.

We had always loved Dad's movies and watched 16-mm copies on weekends at home. Watching him on the screen was also a way of feeling closer to him. We were so proud of him.

When he was on stage, we saw a very different person. He was our dad, but not our dad. On stage and screen, he was super special, bigger than life.

When Dad was at home, he could be one of two people: the loving father who hugged and kissed us, or an angry stranger to stay away from. If he walked in the front door and whistled to us, we ran and embraced him. If he came in with no whistle, we could hear his huge key ring hit the marble entry table and know it was time to head for the hills.

When he returned from long trips when we were very young, we made welcome home signs and put them on the front door. He always brought nice presents for us, but we would have settled for fewer presents and more time with him.

My first marriage broke up after about four years. At that time, I was playing the role of my father—minus the affairs. My second marriage resulted in three beautiful children before my wife left me. Now I have played both roles: I have given pain and had it returned tenfold. My parents have given much to me and I have learned from all I have seen.

My kids and their mother have made mistakes, which I hope we can accept with humor and humanity. I told the boys that one small action always has a chain reaction. And the actions of celebrity offspring are like those ripples in a pond—they get larger and larger and soon are quite disproportionate! That has been something we have all learned the hard way.

We named our fifth son Anthony. It was time for a namesake for the marvelous marble garden statue—which has been such a source of solace to me—that Jerry had imported from Italy.

Anthony could be a little scamp. One of the nannies, Simone, required the boys to be quiet after I had told them goodnight, something Anthony found difficult. Trying to be quiet as a mouse, one night Anthony crept in the kitchen for ice. Simone's sharp ears heard the noise and she asked what he was doing. Barely in school, he nevertheless had a rational answer, "I was quiet," he said, "but the ice was clicking." Even stern Simone couldn't help but laugh.

Anthony has always been articulate, orderly, and *together*. I appreciate his penning his past thoughts in a positive light.

Anthony: *My father was always the strongest person in my life when I was growing up. He was the ultimate role model, the consummate disciplinarian (which at times I wasn't too thrilled about, but respected him for in my own juvenile way, somehow knowing that at the root of discipline is concern of one kind or another) and he was most certainly the king of the household. As a young boy I knew Dad was a very important man, because of the way the house snapped to attention when he walked through the door and the overwhelming respect and admiration he commanded anywhere we went. I didn't know exactly why these things happened, but I always told myself I wanted to be like that when I grew up.*

The friendship bond with my father was and is not like one the average person may envision. We did not grab a couple of fishing poles and go down to the pond to cast for trout on a warm afternoon. I missed out on that. Gary and Ron had enjoyed that type of closeness in the earlier years. It's all very subjective, though. There was nothing to which I could reference my experiences, so my interaction with Dad was in light of my perception of how things were supposed to be.

Dad and I did not spend much time alone together, but I never felt cheated; I still do not, even today. I suppose I was born under a very objective star. The couple of times I was able to go to San Diego for a weekend on our boat with him are among the best memories I have.

Watching Dodger games, driving to the studio for the day to watch production—these are the things that remain with me and are very special. The quality time we spent together may not have been frequent, but it was memorable.

Regardless of the loose talk in the media, internal family politics, and the subjectivity of disgruntled siblings, I can sit here peacefully, and honestly say that Dad has always been a friend to me. Maybe not in the conventional sense, according to society's norm. But there was always a warm embrace when I needed it, or words of encouragement for a school project, or a thoughtful gift for no particular reason. I know he felt guilty for being away so much, and it was difficult for him to talk about it.

Certain individuals pervert the recollection of frequent gift-giving saying, "Oh, he just bought us off because he was away so much." I really don't agree. He expressed himself the best way he knew how, and that was part of it. Somehow I sensed that he hoped we would understand. I always did and was grateful for everything I had.

Another way my father showed his love for us was by kissing his children on the lips. Now, while this may not have been too macho for a seventh grader, it was our greeting and parting expression of affection. With hindsight, especially being the father of two myself, I applaud him for this. My most profound term of endearment is to kiss my kids on the lips. I'll never stop doing that. I love them, and this is something that just feels right.

It did to him, and he wasn't afraid to show it.

Dad's work was always bigger than life to me. I did not understand a lot about it as a child, but I knew he had a very important job.

Try to envision it through a child's eyes: driving up to the magnificent arched gateway of Paramount Pictures, proceeding with a security escort to a giant sound stage, and opening the door to reveal a teaming menagerie of actors, extras, sound and lighting crews, technicians, carpenters, camera operators, script and continuity people, makeup and wardrobe people, messengers, grips, gofers, cronies, and a host of others. And there's my father, busier than a bird-dog, personally giving instructions to practically everyone on the set.

A child's intellect does not break out all the particulars behind this type of authority, but it does perceive the fact that Dad is in charge, and must be a pretty important guy. It made me feel proud.

Holidays, especially Christmastime, were certainly not your average undertaking in our house. Most folks in those days did just fine photographing Christmas festivities with a silent Super 8 movie camera. We had a miniature sound stage set up in the living room. Dad set up his 16-mm sound-on-film camera with floodlights, shotgun microphones, and even live playback with holiday music. Consequently, we have some pretty spectacular mementos to watch and show our children. For the most part, it was a lot of fun. The out-takes are the funniest. Dad staged the "grand entrance" to the living room with all of us shuffling in according to height. (How do you control six boys on Christmas morning with all those presents sitting there? Not very well.) We would fumble through a couple of takes, then let loose. It's great to have those memories captured on film.

One good example from my "not your average dull life" file was a birthday when I was in the second grade, and a dual celebration at Disneyland for Chris and me had been planned. As we struggled over the invitation list, Dad stepped in and instructed us each to invite our whole class. That is exactly what we did. Both classes convened at our Bel Air home and boarded two shiny new Greyhound buses, and off to Disneyland we went. The party was held in a banquet room above Main Street, where I was fortunate enough that day to meet Walt Disney, who stopped in to check on his guests. It was a very special day for all of us.

I suppose I could cite a few instances of sad memories, but I must clear the record and say this much: It seems to be fashionable these days for Hollywood offspring to dredge up past events concerning their parents, sensationalize them, and put them into print. I don't subscribe to this activity. When Homer Smith of Abilene, Texas, pelts Junior on the behind for kicking the cat, it's part of just another day on the farm. But when Jerry Lewis whacks his son for misbehaving, all of a sudden it's world news. The act of children making money by defaming their parents can only be classified as mercenary opportunism. God forbid that show people should be human.

Sure, my father became angry at times. When properly provoked, anyone will. But he was never wild or uncontrollable. Even in the depths of his Percodan addiction, he never made insane gestures, or spoke abusively for no particular reason. (Or if he did, I was not present.) At times he was very irascible, though. Doors slammed and voices were raised, at which point we boys promptly headed for the hills.

The results of Dad's addiction were mostly passive, such as his sleeping on the couch all day. What made me particularly sad was seeing him in pain. I felt the anguish, both physical and emotional, and knew he was taking pills for it. The drugs put great spiritual distance between him and all of us. They did make him especially aloof and unresponsive to us at times. From my standpoint, this was unfortunate because this time period was a very crucial and formative time in my life. But I somehow always managed to rationalize what was happening and didn't look on him acrimoniously. I would be less than honest, though, if I didn't admit that the lack of recognition hurt at times. He was basically in his own world.

I was also saddened by his absence. I always knew and understood he had a demanding job, but nevertheless, I missed him while he was away.

My best and most enduring memories of all of us being together have to be the many trips to San Diego and being on our boat(s). This was pure pleasure for everyone. There were simply no negatives. We went there as a family to have a good time, and we always did. I think that is why I love San Diego so much today. We boys loved to fish, while the adults enjoyed the serenity of just being near the water. My dad and Joe Stabile would go water-skiing, and somewhere in the plan we would work in a harbor cruise or two, and possibly Sea World. It was just a lot of fun.

We also enjoyed Palm Springs, where we had a small house with a beautiful pool and numerous fruit trees we loved to "harvest" in the summer. It was a place to go at various times throughout the year just to get away.

When we were in London while Dad was directing the film One More Time, the sightseeing was wonderful, as was watching the lunar landing. I also recall seeing some crass comics on British television whom we all agreed would never make it to America: Bennie Hill and the Monty Python gang!

In the early 1980s it was rather obvious to all of us, with the exception, perhaps, of Joseph, that a split between our parents was imminent. They had not been together physically for months, and seemed to be almost avoiding any kind of contact with one another. Naturally, we spoke to people who were somewhat in touch with the "grapevine," and certain facts fortified our supposition.

I certainly felt bad for both of my parents, for many reasons: what they had shared together for all those years, what they had built together—what was to come of everything? My version is a trifle different from my brothers', though. Concurrent with my parents' personal difficulties, Sharon and I were at a crucial crossroad in our young lives. We had become engaged, and were discussing the how/when/where of getting married. At this point in time, we were living in the Bel Air house with Mother.

As the divorce climate became more volatile, Sharon and I found ourselves being dragged into a political undertow which was not only forcing us to choose sides, but was also overshadowing any and all notions of our getting married. The irony was just too much to handle.

Sharon and I were unable to make a logical, collected decision as to how to handle the whole issue. Getting out of that environment seemed the only solution open to us, and we took it, thus becoming persona non grata to everyone except my father.

There is quite a bit more to it, but any further commentary along those lines can only be classified as mud-slinging, and I see no useful purpose in bringing any of it up. Subsequently, Sharon and I were married in Las Vegas. The only family members present were Dad, my best man, and his mother, Rae. It was a wonderful, magical wedding we will not forget. I deeply regret that Mom and my brothers were not there. (It has taken some time, but thankfully, most of the scars are healed, and practically all the relationships have been restored.)

For the first three years or so after the divorce, things were downright miserable between Mom, Sharon, and me. But a wise person once said, "It is a mistake to assume we achieve success through success. Much more often, we succeed through failure."

In the same vein, the rapport Sharon and I have with Mother today is such because all three of us have crossed that line between love and contempt, and realized how distasteful it is on the other side, which I believe gives us a greater resolve to ensure that it will never happen again.

In summary, we all went through a very confusing time,

but somehow managed to pull through it. Today, I don't believe there are any active or open wounds on anyone's part. Certain memories of that period aren't particularly pleasant, but we all seem to have a pretty good grasp on what we're doing in life, and how we feel about ourselves—with the exception of Joseph, who is probably the greatest enigma in contemporary family history.

Using the last ten years as an example, I guess you could say my relationship with Dad is much like Halley's Comet: consistent, but closer at some times than at others. I really haven't figured out why. I can't help but think the distance is sometimes planned.

From 1980 to 1982, Sharon and I were always with Dad and had a very good time together. When my brothers began to filter back into the picture after the divorce had settled down, my wife and I were more or less relegated to the wayside, for whatever reason. Since then, things have been generally amenable, but sporadic. My greatest regret in all this is the kids don't see much of him. They know who he is, they get a big kick out of watching him on TV on the weekends, and in their own way, they want to get to know him. Our meetings are simple and pleasant, but not nearly often enough.

I want to add a footnote to Anthony's thoughts. As he mentioned, when he and Sharon were going to get married, it was the year I filed for separation. I asked them to wait until I could get things straightened out. Then Jerry and I could be there and there would be no problems.

Looking back, I am sure that I would not have been anxious to postpone marrying Jerry those many years ago. Asking them to delay their happiness because mine was dissolving was not a wise thing to do. But Sharon's mother had called, asking me to pay for part of the wedding and it was difficult then for me to get funds together, for our money was tied up. I told Anthony to call his father and ask him to pay for part of the wedding, since his balance sheet was far better than mine.

Anthony informed me that Jerry had promised to give

them a big wedding in Las Vegas. I reiterated that I would not be able to come because the separation was too fresh and Jerry would be accompanied by his girlfriend. The kind of pain that involves is raw and indescribable.

The other boys then chose not to attend. I realize that Anthony and Sharon wanted a big wedding; their plans were not made to hurt me. I'll never blame them for going ahead. It was the most exciting time of their lives, and they wanted it to be special.

They married at seven p.m. That same night, the boys took me to Chasen's for dinner and at seven o'clock sharp, we toasted Anthony and Sharon with champagne. Although stories circulated that we were having a whoop-te-do time, the truth is, I was crying: My fifth baby was getting married and I wasn't there. Years later, I cherish the video that takes me to the most important wedding I ever missed.

The years went on. I was pregnant again. With the birth of Joseph, we were eight. These were days when I felt I was going east, looking for a sunset. Jerry was going through horrible changes, and although I was thrilled with the prospect of having another baby, I also had the feeling of being an inconvenience to my husband.

During this pregnancy more than any other, Jerry developed a black belt in sarcasm. The pot at the end of my rainbow felt empty. Yet I kept these feelings inside.

The day of Joseph's baptism, Jerry placed the following note by a photograph of himself holding our baby:

Hold me tight, Dad, not because I'm worried... really... but only because I'm small and I'm sure I'd hurt if I fall...

I remembered that day, and for the next few years I kept Joseph held tightly to me. He was the last baby and would need all the love I could find. I did not want him hurt. I didn't want him to fall into the sadness I was experiencing.

With five big brothers, Joseph had lots of "dads." He also had one of the greatest needs for his real one. During Joseph's formative years, Jerry was rarely home. I recall one night when I was not able to get Joseph to sleep, and I turned on the television. He saw a Schick commercial Jerry had made, pulled up the covers, and announced, "Now that I saw Daddy, I can sleep." And he was satisfied.

Glimpses of humor sprinkled Joseph's childhood. When he had to have an X-ray of his foot, he wanted the doctor who was taking it to autograph it to "My fine-footed friend."

Helping me in the garden one day he noted, "These old tomato plants have roots deeper than Alex Haley's!"

Life for Joseph was different. His response when I told him I was filing for separation was, "Now I won't be able to play golf with my father." But the hurts ran much deeper. He may have been the most devastated victim of our last trying years and divorce. Many of his memories were hurtful; memories that focused on his dad, but spilled into other areas too.

His sense of security was undermined by many events, typical of which was the time Joseph saw his dad on a talk show chatting with Dr. Jonas Salk and Mike Douglas about raising children. Jerry boldly remarked, "I never put my children on hold. I'm always there for them." This was in marked contrast to what had happened a few days earlier, when seventeen-year-old Joseph had wanted to talk to Jerry in person and Jerry had wanted to talk to Joseph on the phone. A crestfallen Joseph tried to equate the TV comment with his recent experience, then he flipped off the TV. He was not quiet about his feelings. I still pray he will emerge strong, able to put the past in its proper place, and with his emotional baggage out of sight and mind.

Every time I heard Jerry expound on his treatment of the boys, I knew that, to a certain degree, he *was* there for the older kids, and I always knew he meant what he was saying. However, *doing* what he was saying was another matter.

Joseph has some angry memories.

Joseph: *I was sixteen years old. My parents had just separated. With my mom and my brother Chris, we entered*

Dad's old bathroom—a place where he spent hours every day when he was home. We were about to find out why. Chris took a large pair of bolt cutters and put them to a lock on a drawer. Next to the lock was a sign, "If anyone plays with this lock, it would create serious trouble for the party involved."

The lock was cut and the drawer opened. It contained several ounces of marijuana, and many prescription drugs.

So that was what he had been doing—not lying on the marble floor to soothe his aching back, as he had said! It was a cheap alibi, from a cheap father. I lost what little respect I had left for the man.

When I was very young (between three and six) I usually saw Dad only at dinner time. The rest of the day was spent with my governess in my own private play yard. That was the only place I was allowed to be a child. The rest of the time, I felt like a trained monkey, a circus freak. My earliest fond memories of Dad were at the dinner table. He was notorious for shaking salt all over the table, sticking carrots in his ears and nose, and smearing brownies all over his teeth. But even then, I knew not to feel secure in my dad's folly. I knew his mood could swing with one wrong move, and it usually did.

Little did anyone know at the time that these mood swings were due to drugs.

The dinner table was mostly a place of fear for my brothers and me. We were to sit quietly, speak only if spoken to, and eat quickly and silently. We had to ask permission to rise. If we happened to ask when Dad was watching television, we were scolded. Many offenses could be committed at the dinner table. By far the worst was walking in front of the television. We were required to go the long way around the large marble table. If we passed in front of the set, we were called to the commander's side, where we were asked, "Are you going to do that again?", If "No, sir" was not spoken quickly enough, we were subjected to a withering look. Sometimes, I couldn't answer, out of sheer fright. This was in the days before remote control, and blocking the screen, even while changing the channel, brought a reprimand.

One of the most fearsome sounds at the table was three taps of the fork on Dad's plate. It was our call to attention if we were too noisy or were not eating fast enough. Needless to say, it is difficult for a child to eat calmly after being ordered to. (And, even as young as I was, I was not exempt from the same treatment as my brothers.) The consequences of not doing as instructed were far worse.

Two fork taps meant punishment would follow dinner.

I was born a mixed-religion breed. Mom is Catholic and Dad Jewish, but he is the last person to observe any Jewish holidays or to go to Temple. All of us were raised, baptized, and confirmed as Catholic. Even though Gary was also confirmed, Dad's parents wanted him to have a bar mitzvah as well. Neither of my parents wanted this, so Dad, being the photographic whiz he is, shot photos of my brother dressed for bar mitzvah in a yarmulke, and holding a Torah, and showed them to his parents. They went to their graves thinking Gary had been bar mitzvahed.

The first eight years of my formal education were at Catholic schools, and I was required to attend services regularly until I was about fourteen. After that I was allowed to stay away frequently.

A very restless child in church, I climbed all over the pew and flipped through the missals hoping to find some good pictures. I was also very good at falling down, hitting my head, and letting out screams. These would quickly be followed by Mother's hand over my mouth.

Anthony still gets needled about the time when, enamored with flushing toilets, he stood on the pew during the service, and, facing backward, loudly announced his intention to flush all the toilets when he got home. Needless to say, Mom was quite embarrassed. She was also thankful she was in Coronado, rather than her home parish.

When I was about twelve, I got to know the ushers in the church and, during Mass, helped collect the offering in a basket on the end of a long pole. One day when nobody was looking I took five dollars out of the basket. I really didn't know what I intended to do with the money, or why I had taken it in the first place. When I got home I learned one of my first lessons in supreme guilt. God was looking down on me and was not happy and I felt it. I think I was a little crazy that night, and couldn't sleep. The very next day I took the money to school, and on my lunch break, put it back in the donation box. But I still felt bad, so I went to confession. After that, I learned you'd better not cross God, or else.

I will never forget my first confession. We were led into the church by my second-grade teacher, and I was petrified of what was going to happen. I thought the wrath of God was going to come down and slay me for whatever bad things I had done. But confession is not an easy subject for a second grader to comprehend. (However, I am not afraid to repent and show God I am sorry for my sins. And God knows, in the past decade, I have done more than my share of sinning.)

When it came time for my first Communion, I had come down with the chicken pox. My classmates went on without me. The next morning at the 9 a.m. Mass, I received my first communion with the family present. That was the first time I ever recall Dad showing up at church.

The other time I remember his being at church was when Mother was in the hospital just before having surgery. We sat back up in the choir loft alone and I was really touched to see Dad actually bow his head and pray like he meant it.

There was only one other occasion when I was present that Dad was anything remotely like religious, and that was at Passover dinner in Las Vegas at the home of the late comedienne Totie Fields. It was her last one. Instead of wearing a yarmulke, Dad wore a Chinese-style beanie hat, and even inserted his fake buck teeth. Totie was laughing out loud, but Mother thought it very insulting.

Totie's husband, Georgie Jessel, said, "It's okay, Patti. I haven't seen her laugh like this in a long time, and she may not be with us much longer." She died a few weeks later. I felt very good about my dad and myself that night. It was a reminder of the good he could do in the world.

After getting my first car, I attended church only on special holidays. In recent years, I haven't gone even then. I know I will have to go to confession and ask forgiveness, but until then, I wear a cross around my neck in a way that makes me feel close to God. In times of personal despair, I find great comfort in reading the Bible.

Patti's mother, Mary Calonico, with Patti and brother Joseph.
Credit: Patti Lewis Collection

Young Patti playing the accordion at a family picnic. *Credit: Patti Lewis Collection*

Patti playing the accordion in
the summer of 1940.
Credit: Patti Lewis Collection

Promotional picture sent to Jerry with note. (Inset) Patti's
first promotional picture. *Credit: Patti Lewis Collection*

Promotional cutouts of Patti.
Credit: Patti Lewis Collection

Patti with brother Joe. *Credit: Patti Lewis Collection*

Ted's promotional picture sent to Patti with note.
Credit: Patti Lewis Collection

Patti singing with Ted Fio Rito's band.
Credit: Patti Lewis Collection

Patti as teenager with band. *Credit: Patti Lewis Collection*

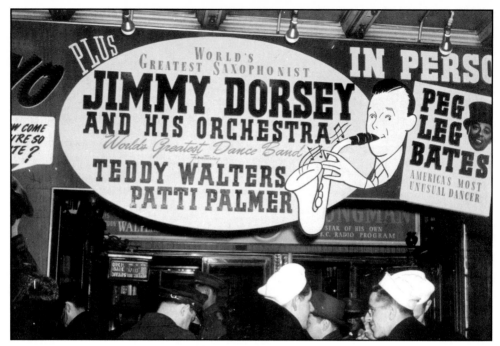

Jimmy Dorsey's promotional sign, featuring Patti. *Credit: Patti Lewis Collection*

Patti (left center) with the Swingles. *Credit: Patti Lewis Collection*

Young Jerry's promotional shot, sent to Patti with note.
Credit: Patti Lewis Collection (Courtesy James Kollar Studios)

Dean and Jerry. (Courtesy Ray Fisher) *Credit: Patti Lewis Collection*

Dean and Jerry. (Courtesy Ray Fisher) *Credit: Patti Lewis Collection*

Dean and Jerry with Joe DiMaggio and Marilyn Monroe. *Credit: Patti Lewis Collection*

Dean and Jerry with Jimmy Durante. *Credit: Patti Lewis Collection*

Dean and Jerry in the
"Colgate Comedy Hour"
(1952).
Credit: Patti Lewis Collection

Dean and Jerry with
Burt Lancaster.
Credit: Patti Lewis Collection

Jerry and Patti with Gary at the Atlantic City Boardwalk. *Credit: Patti Lewis Collection*

Jerry and Gary. *Credit: Patti Lewis Collection*

Jerry and Patti at the wedding of Dean and his second wife, Jeannie.
Credit: Patti Lewis Collection

(Upper and lower) Jerry celebrating his two-million-dollar deal with Paramount with guests Ronald Reagan and Edward G. Robinson.

Guests Eddie Cantor and Louella Parsons celebrate with Jerry.
Credit: Patti Lewis Collection

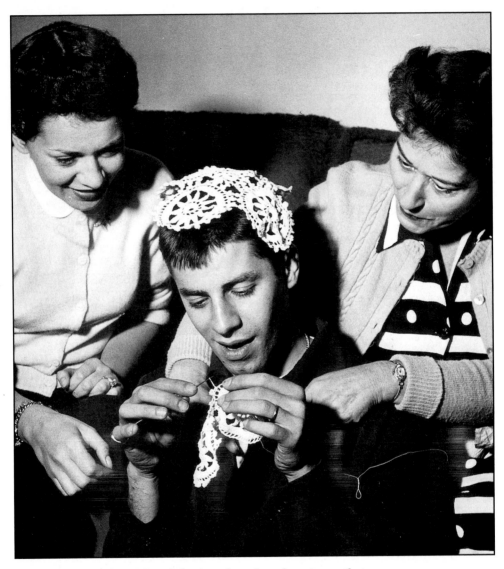

Patti and her mother, Mary Calonico, show Jerry how to crochet.
Credit: Patti Lewis Collection

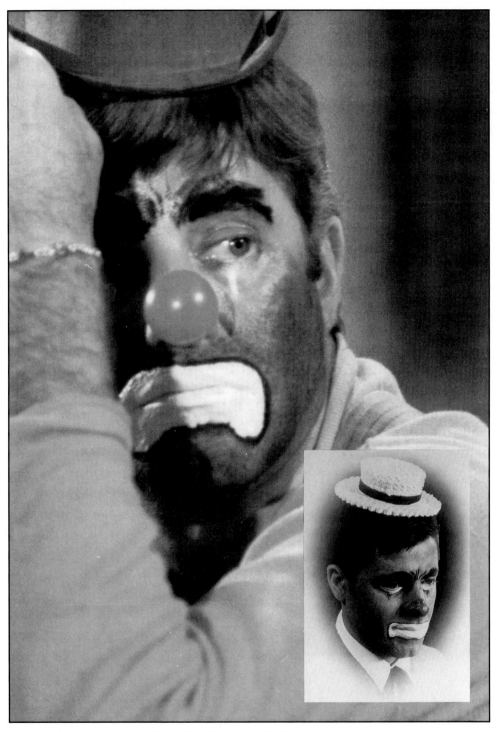

Jerry as the sad clown in *Three Ring Circus. Credit: Patti Lewis Collection*

Jerry as the Nutty Professor. *Credit: Patti Lewis Collection*

"Hold me tight, Dad, not because I'm worried..
really... But only because I'm small and I'm sure
I'd hurt if I fell.. But that's the only reason
   I say,'Hold me tight...' I'm quite aware of the
      heart and mind you have for me.. I can feel it now
as you hug me... and I know how much LOVE and warmth
      you're going to provide for me... I'm really a very
         lucky baby... If I would have come to another house
            with other people, they might have had lots of love
               and care as a child, and I might just have had to
                  do without... I'm so very grateful and happy you're
my dad.. Your arms hold me warm and hug me with
LOVE and I'm at peace with my new world.. So please
   don't worry or fret where I'm concerned.. 'cause I'm
      starting out with all the equipment that's really
necessary... Your love, your embrace, and your care..
Yet with my secure feelings, I can't help but feel
   a little sorry for you, Dad, 'cause I think you would
      have loved it too."

(The day of Joseph's baptism, Jerry placed this note beside a photograph of himself holding the baby.)

Jerry holding Joseph, the last child the couple was to have.
Credit: Patti Lewis Collection

Family portrait (painted by Fred Williams). *Credit: Patti Lewis Collection*

Family Christmas photo. *Credit: Patti Lewis Collection*

Patti and her six sons, Ron, Gary, Joseph, Chris, Anthony, and Scott.
Credit: Patti Lewis Collection

Family wearing spacesuits provided by the studio after Jerry's film, *Visit to a Small Planet.*
Credit: Patti Lewis Collection

Patti and Jerry with President Harry S Truman. *Credit: Patti Lewis Collection*

Jerry with President and Mrs. Richard Nixon. *Credit: Patti Lewis Collection*

Patti and Jerry with President John F. Kennedy. *Credit: City News Bureau*

Patti and Jerry with Governor John Connally of Texas. *Credit: Patti Lewis Collection*

Patti and President Jimmy Carter. *Credit: Patti Lewis Collection*

Patti and Jerry at an award ceremony. (Inset) Jerry and Dean with Frank Sinatra.
Credit: Patti Lewis Collection

Patti with Lori Caldwell. *Credit: Patti Lewis Collection*

Patti with Phil Donahue. *Credit: Patti Lewis Collection*

Patti with Dr. Michael DeBakey.

Patti with Bishop Fulton Sheen. *Credit: Patti Lewis Collection*

Patti and family. *Credit: Patti Lewis Collection*

I do intend to attend church again soon. Mother sings in the choir and I am ashamed not to have seen her there more.

It was very difficult to have a solid relationship with Dad as I grew up due to his constant travel. However, there were many times he provided pleasure for me when he was home. Although he was strict, he taught me how to be an excellent baseball player, as well as a golfer. I am sorry, however, that he seldom took the time to watch me play in a Little League game, other than running in for a quick 16-mm moment, or actually take me out to play golf on a big course. Even though paternal influences were lacking at times, and I was scared of him at other times, the things he did shaped my life in a way which made me learn most of the lessons a child needs to learn.

My mother had more influence on my childhood than anyone else. Whether Dad was home or not, Mom was always there for me. No matter how bad things got, she was my number-one supporter and my best friend. As I was attending grade school, Mom taught me the ways of the Lord, and helped me grow with God.

I will never forget her kindness. She would have a Slurpee or candy bar waiting for me every day after school when she came to pick me up. It was such a simple gesture, but sometimes those gestures are the most important. Mom gave me what I needed most as a child—constant support, true love, and lots of hugs.

As I grew, Dad was around less and less with each passing year, but I always had the love of my mom to fall back on. Throughout the years, that love never waned, it only grew, and I could feel the welcome spot which she held for me in her heart. Through all the trials and tribulations of adolescence, Mom was there for me. For better or worse, she was the lone beacon of sensitivity, caring, and rationality in my life. While Dad showed little or no support for me during those formative years, my mom helped me through the tumultuous times of adolescence, and helped me come out with a good head on my shoulders.

Growing up, I frequently said I was going to be the one who would follow in Dad's footsteps. My interest in acting started when I was about eight and performed in a school play. In the eighth grade, I performed one of Dad's skits in the school's annual talent show. All during high school, I took various bits from my dad's acting and put it with my own efforts. I excelled in drama class, and I can directly attribute that to Dad's influence.

My mom has always told me she had wanted to have one last baby, and that she had the love to go through with it. If it had not been for that love, I would not be here today. On a grander scale, the little things which my mom did for me were special. I never went to school hungry, because she always had breakfast waiting for me in the morning, a breakfast she had prepared herself, even though we had a hired cook downstairs.

My mom and I also shared many days at the bowling alley, and she taught me well. She has touched my life in so many wonderful ways, it's impossible to name them all here. But I can safely say that her constant presence and love has been the most meaningful part of my life.

It was painful to see Dad hurting Mom through the entire process of their divorce. This is a woman who gave nothing but love, and did not deserve such pain. Although I missed Dad after he left and it did hurt, it was not as bad as it might have been had I felt he had been a proper dad in the first place. I really had little to lose when he left except for the fear that he frequently instilled in me.

Being the youngest in the family, I was often the brunt of teasing. It didn't feel too good at the time, but now that I am grown, I understand and hold no grudges.

The brother who stands out in my mind as always being there for me was Gary. Although I probably spent less time with him than with any of the other brothers, I still feel a strange, special bond with him. I am so proud of what he has done in his life, and if I had to choose a role model, it would not be my dad, but my brother Gary.

I have never known anyone quite like Mom, and I'm sure I never will. I have never met anyone so pure in heart and soul. She possesses a heart of gold, and could never feel anger or hatred toward anyone. Mom is kind, giving, and charitable. Her work with local charitable organizations has taken up weeks of her time in years past. She believes no sacrifice is too great if it is to help another human being.

She treated all of us, even my dad, with extreme compassion and love. Mother was always there to forgive and forget. At the same time, she acted as a buffer between my dad, the evils of the world, and me, protecting me from much harshness, and for that, I will be forever grateful.

Dad could have promised me the world with his immense wealth, but I would willingly trade it in a second for an ounce of what Mom has given me. Were it not for her, I might never have survived adolescence—and she did the same for my brothers as well. No matter how bad things got, she was always there.

In summation, if there is anyone in this world that is owed a vote of thanks, or even just the tip of a hat, it is Mom. She is special.

When the divorce was final, I went through the stages of wondering about what would have happened if things had been different. I had tried to live a Christian life by God's laws and had tried to pass my peace, thoughts, and teaching on to my children and Jerry. Except for Gary, the boys had all had Catholic educations, and one of my greatest joys was having my sons with me in church. They are true gifts from God.

If I have fallen short of what I should have done, it is only because I did not know another way, not because I gave up. I know I have taught my sons to see good in people first, and not to be negative before knowing all the facts because there are two sides to every situation.

For years, I could not bear the thought of giving up such an exciting life as I had had as the wife of a celebrity. Then, as time progressed, the excitement was replaced by a need for survival. I finally grew up at the age of fifty, and was shocked to realize that I had taken so much grief for so long, feeling all the while that I didn't deserve any better.

It was then I learned that the bitter has an amazing way of making you better, if you are willing to change, that no problem is so big that it cannot be solved by a good miracle. The miracle—of courage to go on even against odds as high as seven to one—happened in me!

He who loses wealth loses much; he who loses a friend loses more; but he who loses courage and faith loses all. The price was not too high. I took a faltering step of faith and put my life in the hands of my loving God.

In Proverbs 7:1, the *Living Bible* says: "My sons, keep God's words, and treasure His commandments within you."

In Psalms 7:1, it says, "I am depending on you, O Lord, my God."

Is it surprising that "seven to one" is significant to me?

Chapter 6

In 1947, I had not seen my good friend, Gilda Maiken Anderson, for quite a few years, not since high school. Our careers had taken separate directions. Her group, the Skylarks, was singing with Jimmy Dorsey, my former band leader. Walking back to our hotel in New York, we spotted each other. Glad to be together again, we had a lot of catching up to do. She knew that I had left Dorsey and that Jerry and I were married.

Gilda asked, "Why did you marry Jerry, of all people? He's loud, homely, and very juvenile in every way. I've read about him. You are so different, Patti. You are beautiful, shy, and one classy lady—and there have been plenty of other men in your life."

Although this happened a long time ago, both of us remembered my immediate answer, "He loves me very much and he makes me laugh."

The year was 1947. Gary was barely two years old. Martin and Lewis were becoming "news."

That night, I left Gilda and returned to the hotel to join Jerry for the show that evening. Loving music as I did, I would sit through his comedy acts and try to become engrossed with the background recordings he used for impersonations. The rhythm and beat and instrumental arrangements would all too soon be overwhelmed by Jerry's onstage clowning. I couldn't help myself. His classic facial contortions and his trademark gesturing played right into my emotional system. That kind of a response was inevitable, even from those who wanted to remain unimpressed. We all laughed until we cried.

Jerry had a unique way of forging a lasting impression on the comedy department of your brain. Phrases, words, or word couplets he extracted from conversations or performances soon found their way into movies or became marketing tools for aggressive merchandisers. Jerry plucked a phrase I had uttered—Are you for real?—from the moment I had been introduced to him. The audience began to anticipate the question, though they were seldom able to predict where it would pop up in a Lewis-Martin routine.

When I was pregnant with our last son, Joseph, Jerry had a song written called, "Think Pink." In a surge of acceptance, the whole country latched onto the phrase. After five sons, we speculated that our friends thinking "pink" thoughts couldn't hurt. I. Magnin, in the Los Angeles Wilshire District, transformed its entire baby department with shades of pink. They had gorgeous bouquets of pink carnations placed on the counters. Pink dresses and toys headed the racks and tables.

During that time, the Jimmy Durantes gave me a magnificent, baby shower. Everything was decorated in pink. Marjorie even had cascades of pink flowers floating in the pool. The gifts were definitely baby-girl presents.

When I asked Jimmy where he had adopted the nickname, "Schnozzola," he pulled out some childhood memories of when he was made fun of and laughed at... until he literally cried. Then he recalled a little kid who had once told him that he had a big nose, too. After seeing Jimmy on TV, the boy decided it really was not so life-threatening, and started asking his friends to call him "Schnozzy." Jimmy had little namesakes all over the world, and that unusually sculpted nose was not the only reason.

Our children loved Jimmy, and had since they first met him on a Christmas visit to his home. It made us sad to see him confined to a wheelchair, but happy when we thought he was recovering. He was a gentle friend.

Jerry was asked to participate in the 31st Annual Academy Awards presentation at the RKO Pantages Theatre in Hollywood. This was a real honor for Jerry, since he was joining the ranks of the other hosts, such as Bob Hope, David Niven, Sir Laurence Olivier, Tony Randall, and Mort Sahl. Quite an impressive list of performers. I was proud of my husband's class and composure as I sat through those awards which attract such a huge audience of celebrities and television viewers. Jerry has never received an Oscar, but I give him my highest award for a job well-done.

That same year two young actresses were representing the U.S. State Department on a goodwill tour in Japan. They saw several blue-eyed, homeless orphans wandering unattended. There had been a recent typhoon and their hearts were touched into action. They brought eleven home. The women, Sarah O'Meara and Yvonne Fedderson, launched a crusade to plan and raise funds to assist more children who were victims of the short affairs between American G.I.s and their Japanese liaisons. The next year, they incorporated. Their work resulted in several orphanages in Japan and a subsequent hospital and care facility in Vietnam.

These two ladies had a goal of someday having a real "Children's Village" for abused youngsters. Many of my friends were active in a local chapter. We all worked toward their great spiritual and humanitarian goal.

Eighteen years later, in 1977, Abigail Van Buren and I were honored as the organization's "Women of the Year." My award was especially meaningful to me because my son, Ron, made my introduction.

The inscription on the award read:

Patti's whole life is testimony to her love and concern for children, all children, and it is this love which prompts International Orphans, Inc. to offer her its coveted "Woman of the Year" award this year. Her untiring dedication to children's causes in such a busy life is an inspiration to us all.

Awards were not new to Jerry or to me, but this particular one, from an organization which still remains active and vital, was particularly special.

The span of years between Jerry's superb performance

at the Oscars and my gift of recognition were both troubled and treasured. Our lives were full. Jerry's films and appearances kept him further away for longer periods of time. I had the children at home at various stages. The boys went through periods that defied my assumption of what kids were all about. With Jerry gone, I struggled for right answers, and to keep them happy.

When it was suggested that Jerry and I see a therapist, we went. However, Jerry told the doctor to teach me to live with him just the way he was.

After the breakup with Dean, I felt we had become closer than before. I had shared Jerry with Dean for ten years, and Dean's philosophy had been that the wives should not socialize together. We respected that. At the same time, it appeared to the outside world that Betty and I were at odds. We were not. We remained good friends.

Yet the relationship had its swings. There were times I was so loaded down with gifts from Jerry that I could have started a jewelry store. At other times, he was distant. It became increasingly hard to find common ground other than the children. And on that subject, we were often divided.

Gary went through hell when he was in the service in Korea. He and Elvis Presley were drafted at the same time, at the height of their careers. We were proud of him, but concerned about the effects the experience would have on a kid raised in Bel Air.

During his stint in the army, Gary's career and family had been put on hold. (He had a wife and baby.) While he was away, music was undergoing a major transition. Then, on his return, his wife could not accept the changes in him and the marriage was dissolved.

Jerry could not understand what was going on with his oldest son. When Gary turned to drugs, Jerry refused to acknowledge the reasons behind this. He turned our son's pictures against the walls, or jerked them down in anger. There was no outward empathy. As a wife, I had to believe that somewhere within he felt for Gary's situation, but all we saw was rage. Consequently, that was a period of little laughter and much pain.

I was torn between love for them both. I could not allow a floundering son not to be loved by his mother. He came over often after Jerry had sent him away, and we talked things out. He wanted to be loved and surrounded by family. Thank God, Gary has always been a survivor—something he had to have inherited from both of his parents.

I remember another incident regarding Gary with a happier ending. One year he got into a scrape with two old "biddies" (his description). These women claimed he had banged into their car as he was pulling out of a parking space on the street. One initiated a warrant for his arrest after noting his license plate number. Soon Gary was picked up by the area police and taken to jail. It was hot copy for the newspapers: JERRY LEWIS' SON ARRESTED.

Gary had told us what transpired. We were working it out when the telephone rang. A man said, "Patti?"

"Yes."

The voice asked me to hold just a minute. "The wop wants to talk to you."

I could not imagine who was on the other end of the line. Suddenly, Frank Sinatra picked up the phone and said, "Hey, dago. This is Francis."

We chit-chatted for a few minutes, then he asked how we were, especially Gary. He asked if there was any way he could help. That was a side of Frank a lot of people never saw. When he was your friend, especially as one Italian to another, he cared. He made us all appreciate those who are concerned and who take the time to let you know they're there if needed. Gary's situation worked out to everyone's satisfaction.

Jerry was a master at candidly acting out personal vignettes about three areas of real life: relationships, situations, and predicaments. They form the backbone of his comedy. He nurtured many relationships and wrote volumes on how he felt. I tried to understand what he was saying, beyond the words, when I read the notes he sent me; the "I luv you's" written across my makeup mirror at home; and the longer messages I found on my desk.

At times I found him five parts philosopher, one part humanist, ten parts deep thinker, one part spiritual, fifty parts comedian, twelve parts unpredictability, and twenty-one parts everything else. In 1966, one late summer afternoon, I found the following and took it to the garden to read:

To ask how deeply I feel is like asking, "Where is God?"

We can answer with nothing more than "if's" and "maybe's."

In other words, the answers are really intangibles, yet I'm going to attempt to answer one of them to the best of my knowledge and awareness.

My feelings, where my wife is concerned, are very deep and very sacred... She is the very reason I live... for she is the only reason I know that makes living worth anything... and the boys that she produced for me are equally worth it, but one day they'll leave and then there will be only us...

She is the first human thing that has ever cared about me or for me... Oh, there were little dogs and little boys and a few beings that cared, but not enough that I could have survived.

It was only when she came into my life that I realized I had a life to live... I was always made to feel that I was given a case of breath out of pity... It was as though someone said, "We have plenty, give him some."

Then I knew I had to make good and be someone, or something a little better than those that gave me an occasional handout...

As I got older, I didn't much care about being better than them anymore... I just cared about staying alive and getting some degree of respect as a human thing on God's Earth... I knew he didn't mean to have anyone just exist... but he meant for us all to have a meaning and a purpose.

I have to try to get my thoughts put in the proper place so I can put things down that really count!

Now then, if my wife was the first to care and to really

treat me like a human being with love and warmth and the like... the big question is, "How could I have treated this special being as I have?"

My answer that I find coming is...

After so many years of being made to feel like nothing... I guess I worked on being something so much more than nothing... that I found myself making the real somethings around me nothing in the haste that drove me to be something... The responsibility of taking care of the loves I had always had made me feel like, "Why should I care for what one day will discard me anyway?"

I don't know if that's the case, but it sounds right... and coming from someone who loves those tremendous loves as I do, it certainly confuses me, too...

My constant silence, I think, has been fear... of what my love would think of what I've done... fear of doing the wrong thing... and losing the respect I have always felt I got from her... to be placed in the position of being disrespected and disregarded again has always knotted up my insides so badly that silence seemed the only way to avoid the possibility of rejection... very often my hiding was part and parcel of that fear... The feeling of being nothing again, or being looked at with disdain, has, for as long as I can remember, been tearing me up inside... And those tears have come out looking like torment... Well, tormented I am, and have been, and pray one day soon I won't know the feeling anymore...

My wrapping myself up so completely in my work helped for a while, but the "ego" that came across was never there... I have none. But I work desperately at displaying "ego" to cover the real emptiness I know is inside...

As a director I have found infinite peace... because I am to so many... an authority, a man who knows, and not someone who is treated with "pity" or "charity"... That's the biggest reason for the love of creativity I have, for a man is free when he is creating.

Not just creating "funny" by way of the mask I wear, but by making others the puppets... and making them stand out front for a change... The feeling of "behind the camera" feels safe, and warm, and special, and certain... "Out front" has been very hard and trying for me... and for the first time in my life I think I can honestly admit... I hated doing it and I still do... The happiness that seemed to appear from standing "in one" was nothing more than getting a general acceptance from a lot of people who care at the moment... But "at the moment" isn't enough for me anymore...

I need all the care I can get all the time... and I only seem to be able to get that from my love, my wife...

I don't ever want to appear "indifferent" to my wife... but that appearance, too, I think is just hoping not to be a burden and an annoyance to her... I just can't remember ever being anything but an annoyance... and when I'm told I'm not, I can't seem to recognize that is possibly the case.

I don't like to hide and run... I want to be free to go and do as any other man does...

I know I need help... but I really believe the help will come from within... as soon as I can place things in their right positions...

Admitting to "hating performing" might help me adjust sooner... Admitting the love I have for writing and direction will, I'm sure, take me out of the depths of my depression... and will ultimately take me into the realm of peace and contentment.

I want to talk more, I want to communicate more... I want to say so much, and get help from her, I want so much to scream the things that tug away at my heart and my soul... And when I try, the hurt is so strong, and deep, and festered that I clam up, and the relief I want doesn't come...

Now to bury that grief... I find someone who has equally as much or more than I so that I can be the helping hand... For if I can help, then my hurts can't be so bad... How much trouble can I have, if I'm listening to someone else's? And for years I made that a practice... to give of myself only to forget I needed more giving than anyone...

I don't think I have always been aware of that fact... I really wanted to share and give and be charitable... but there's that word again... charitable... I should have known better. For "charity" was the one thing that started my life wrong...

I wasn't entitled to charity by those people when I was so very young... I was entitled to all the love and care all little lives should get... But how long did I have to wait to realize "charity" shouldn't deal with the ones we love... They should only get the real "love" and nothing more... and give "charity" to strangers in need... Period! (And they should be picked carefully!)

I'm trying to feel "God" in me and maybe with his help we can push out the torment... and place the "alive" of a being, back where it was taken from...

With it all I am a very lucky man... to have found the real, right, and perfect human being to spend my years with.

I want so much to do the right thing to keep her straight and happy and healthy...

When she is ill, the reaction to it isn't any different than when the spike is forced into the vampire's heart... it's the only emotional thing that can kill me, and that's when she hurts... or when I've caused her pain... but my intentions are never to hurt her, never to do her a moment's pain... Never to create a frown on her lovely face... Why those things happen are a complexity to us both... And I will serve myself from here on in as a student of care and concern and caution as to how she gets treated and how I allow much of my feelings to affect her...

I can only answer "God" honestly, and he knows my worth and my intentions, I have no fear of his wrath... for I know he knows I'm basically good, and fine, and honorable when it comes to my love and my soul for her...

I have no guilt about what I have done thru my blindness... I only have guilt for the things I might have avoided doing... If I had just put... "First things first."

I will try!

And "God" knows my heart is talking, not the typewriter.

No one will be surprised to learn I was filled with tears during and after reading those words. I agreed it was not his typewriter, but his heart that was doing the talking.

Nonetheless, situations and predicaments were legion at home as they were in his routines. One that occurred in 1965 was serious, and its implications were far-reaching.

Jerry had a closing routine at one of his shows in Las Vegas that was staged so that, at the end, he would tell the audience and show them how exhausted he was. Unfortunately, he would say, he had nothing left to give them. He would then start off stage, leap to the top of a grand piano, do a forward double cartwheel and fall flat on his back to the stage floor. It was more than a crowd-pleaser.

On March 20, he hit the floor so hard he could barely rise. He forced himself up, gingerly moving through the curtain. He knew he was injured. His back throbbed with pain. The doctors examined him and prescribed a painkiller. Jerry had no qualms about taking the medication. After all, the doctors were professionals. Sometimes the Percodan helped; sometimes it did not. When it hurt more than usual, he increased his dosage.

I saw a change in him at home. We sympathized. He tried all forms of cures, but... the show must go on. Sometimes I noticed that the more he was in pain, the harder he worked. To the Percodan were added Norodan and Valium. Then he would have another headache or complain of a bump on his head. He hurt his finger. He broke his wrist. Something was always wrong. Later I understood when you are under high dosages of medication, you are not responsible for all your actions.

His quest for relief took him literally around the world. I had calls from him in Sweden, England, France, and other countries, when he would admit, discouraged, that there were no answers. We knew there was a chip out of his spine. We didn't know just how puzzled the doctors were about what to do for him.

The years passed and I never knew how many prescriptions he filled. I just knew he easily numbed out and he did not act like himself. He was irritable and impatient—more than we had ever seen. At times, the kids, who used to be excited about making signs to welcome him home, fled when he pulled into the driveway.

The drugs became an addiction. Not that Jerry had planned it that way. Quite the contrary, but his need to kill the pain increased dramatically. He took up to a dozen pills during a day.

Other symptoms surfaced and compounded his pain. He lost the feeling in one hand, and there was pain in the other. One of his eyes was affected, and the discomfort spread throughout his body.

Jerry has always loved knowledge. He would ask questions and read medical books and talk to more doctors. There were always questions and no answers. Often he was told he would just have to live with pain. He would come home and say to me sharply, "I live with it... what do they think I am doing?"

He got second opinions and third opinions. Then there were more opinions, friends' advice, and home remedies. Again, relief was more than a swallow away.

Through the telethons, Jerry and I had developed a nice rapport with the famed heart surgeon, Dr. Michael DeBakey. He was very kind to us. Knowing Jerry was suffering, he invited us to his clinic in Houston in 1970. There he wisely advised Jerry to get off the Percodan. But the pain crowded out the suggestion.

On our wedding anniversary in 1973, Jerry contemplated suicide. He says it was the sound of our boys laughing that jolted him back to reality. Still, the reality of the pain persisted, and was taking a greater toll.

It took me a long time to understand how anyone could arrive at suicide. However, if all the layers of hope are slowly stripped away, possibly Jerry thought there was nothing left to kill. How I thank God that "merry hearts do well like a medicine." The kids really saved his life.

The press had a heyday writing about Jerry's addictions. The headlines in the tabloids had him, "finished, dying, out of telethons forever." Again, he has proved them wrong.

Continuing tests, mylograms, and new therapies did not help. I worried, but worry does not lessen pain, either.

It was not until after the telethon in 1978, when he

was receiving injections of Xylocaine in his spine, that Jerry agreed to return to Houston. On arrival, his preliminary X-rays showed a golf-ball-sized ulcer in his stomach which had gone undetected.

Jerry was taken off all drugs and for several days was unaware of what was taking place. I recall one time when there were eleven doctors in his room. I also remember, with great joy, when, after days of sedation, he woke up. He had color in his cheeks, and he looked at me with a twinkle I had not seen in thirteen years. He spoke clearly. "Did you ever hear about a born-again Jew? You're looking at one." He later exclaimed, "My God! They found the answer."

He truly felt born again—free from severe pain and the dreaded after-effects of painkillers.

Our time in the hospital was made more pleasant by Dr. DeBakey and his wife, who made soups and special dishes and brought them in for us.

After Jerry was cleared of the drugs, Dr. DeBakey invited him to go and watch a heart surgery. Jerry did, and photographed much of it. Two days later, he did a performance that included a surgery.

On another of our visits, one of the DeBakey associates was doing a heart and asked if I wanted to watch. I went up into the observation booth. The very next day the man was up walking around in the recovery area, still hooked up to some tubes, but he looked wonderful. Miracles are normal for that surgical team.

I had a special experience while staying with Jerry at the hospital. In the room next to his, in a very secluded section of the hospital, Bishop Fulton Sheen was a patient. After Dr. DeBakey introduced us, I frequently saw the bishop walking about the area in his pajamas and robe.

One day I was doing needlepoint while Jerry was sleeping, and the bishop came in. He said he would like to visit, so we went to his room so our talking wouldn't disturb Jerry. He was such a dear man, I was mesmerized. When I heard he was going to say Mass at six the next morning, I said I would be there. He kindly said, "No, you need your rest. I'll pray for you."

I flew back to Los Angeles on the same plane with Bishop Sheen. He worked on an up-coming speech while I sat by the window, reflecting on life-and-death issues; thanking God Jerry had survived again, and wondering just what was in the future.

When we deplaned, the bishop couldn't find his hat. I reminded him that he hadn't been wearing one when we boarded, so he surmised he must have left it in the men's room in Houston. He joked that he had a way of leaving a trail of hats behind him.

Chapter 7

A couple of agents were standing around talking about how difficult it can be to get entertainers to do fund-raising events. The question was raised, "How do you get Jerry Lewis to do a benefit?" The answer came in unison, "Ask him!"

It was that simple to get Jerry to agree to help people with physical needs. His efforts to make a difference to those with muscular disorders started even before his first one-station attempt in New York, and spanned tens of years before developing into the huge "love network" of today.

However, Jerry's complex, compulsive, and multidirectional personality was never more evident than in his years of telethoning. In fact, one of the telethon floor directors described him as "a contagion of deeply penetrating emotions." Telethon time was his ultimate, emotional roller-coaster ride.

Yet these very emotions drive him to do what he loves best—help kids, raise money, and make people laugh, especially the people whose kids still need the crutch Jerry supposedly shed when he wrote about the sacrifice he had made for his "other kids" in 1978:

The roughest sacrifice I had to make, or chose to make, was neglecting my wife and sons, so that I'd have time for "My kids." That was fine, then, because of *my* being crippled. I am whole now, therefore much good work will still be done, but that work now is for the dystrophic child... and my ability and desire to abandon "my crutch" can only be by placing "my kids" and the ones I fathered, in first position, along with their mother.

I believe he really meant those words at the time, and I tried to live by promises rather than explanations. Jerry made many of both.

The sacrifice or driving desire of which Jerry wrote never surprised me. Often Jerry's eyes would fill with tears when we encountered a handicapped child on the street. The tears were genuine. In fact, our whole family has pieces of caring for those kids tucked in our souls.

Chris, in Las Vegas for the 1991 telethon, told me how hard it is each year to learn that some of the dystrophic children he had come to care about were no longer there. Especially hard for him to deal with was the story of a family from Oregon. Their second son had been a past poster child, and one of his favorites. In 1991, he was gone. Two of his brothers with the same diagnosis are awaiting a cure. Time is running out. So the star-studded, entertaining spectacular called "MDA's Jerry Lewis Telethon" represents a valid premise, and it raises millions of dollars.

In Jerry's 1963 book, *Being a Person,* he wrote some stirring words:

Smile at cripples...
Cripples won't be as
Crippled if you do.
Have pity, have mercy, have faith...
Try harder!

Try harder he did, and he continues to make that same effort. I know his motives have been questioned, but the love he has for "his kids" should never be doubted. Much of the criticism stems from the fact that more than a half-billion dollars has been raised and there is still no cure. The criticism that he plays on people's sympathy and uses pity for pennies—or dollars—or multimillions of dollars—continues.

When we first started out, people with disabilities were called "cripples." Words like "handicapped" or even "challenged" are more accepted today. But what has not changed is Jerry's intention, which was never to degrade or offend anyone's sensitivities. His kids participate for a life-saving purpose, no matter how they are described. Someday the cure *will* be found for those who suffer from the forty-plus related disorders called Muscular Dystrophy by continuing research. It is not possible to predict when a breakthrough will occur. Advancement is encouraging, though the process appears slow.

I salute Robert A. Jones, a *Los Angeles Times* writer, for his column on the 1991 telethon. It sums up the wonder of these events and puts the issues in perspective.

Jerry's Kids: It's a Pity But It Works

Sometime around the 17th hour of the Jerry Lewis telethon, I tuned in. I was looking for signs of pity. "Pity," as you perhaps know, is the crime of which the telethon stood accused. Over the weekend, a group of former poster kids for the Muscular Dystrophy Assn. took to the streets to demand that Lewis be yanked from the telethon because he uses pity to solicit money.

This was intriguing. Jerry Lewis had committed a new offense. He was not just politically incorrect, he was emotionally incorrect.

Over the years, charity leaders have been accused of many sins, from running away with the donation box to living high on the hog. But the pity thing was something new.

In effect, Lewis was charged with a crime of the heart. It implied that he had lost his usefulness to the muscular dystrophy cause because his attitudes had grown dated. The marchers talked much about his frequent use of the words *cripple* and *cursed*.

Clearly, these accusations stung. So threatened was Lewis by the anti-pity committee that he opened the telethon with a denial of their charges. "Please," he said to the marchers, "I'm begging for survival."

You had to be impressed by the power of the pity thing. So while others went to the beach on Labor Day, I sat in the gloom of my den, scrutinizing the Lewis telethon for moral error.

If you've never watched the telethon, I would recommend it. You will be witnessing one of the last artifacts of the 1950s. It is a show that could have been produced by the Godfather, with one Vegas lounge singer following another.

And as to the central question: Yes, pity is everywhere in this show. The Jerry Lewis telethon is a universe constructed entirely of pity. Between the lounge acts come appearances by the suffering victims, and someone cries on camera about every three minutes.

This year's national poster kid, Drew Johnson, is shown at home on videotape. Drew's dad appears on the tape, and soon he is crying. Then Drew's mom cries. The camera shifts to Drew, who looks clear-eyed at the viewers and says, "I love you."

Then Lewis sings a tribute to the late Sammy Davis, Jr., who made many appearances on the telethon. Lewis gets halfway through the first song before he breaks down.

Next, we switch to the Los Angeles poster kid, who appears onstage dressed in black tie and seated in his kid-sized wheelchair. He is asked to demonstrate the mobility of his chair. Smiling, he does a wheelie. The camera pans to members of the audience, who all are shedding tears.

But if you watch long enough, you will begin to realize that something phenomenal is taking place. The pity is translating into money, big buckets of money. Every hour, the telethon's tote board shows another $5 million in donations. By the 18th hour, the total has reached $39 million.

And that's just the little folks. The corporate contributions are tallied separately. Every few minutes, a corporate vice-president walks onto the stage with a check for Lewis. Harley-Davidson forks over $2.1 million. Anheuser-Busch follows with $5.2 million. A national group of firefighters produces $8.5 million.

So, sure enough, it turns out Jerry Lewis is emotionally incorrect. It's my guess that his telethon has outlasted all others for the very reason that it learned to trade in pity more efficiently than the others.

The question is this: As long as the emotional currency translates into the real currency of cash, who cares? Before it was all over, the final tote board had hit $45,071,857, and the corporate contributions just about matched that. Figure roughly $80 million for the day's work.

That's a chunk. Let's ask this last question of the marchers who would like to see Lewis drummed out of the telethon: Just who is going to keep this cash machine going? Who is going to stand on that stage for 21-1/2 hours, maintain emotional correctness, never indulge in cashable pity, and still pull in $80 million for muscular dystrophy?

Sean Penn? Sinead O'Connor? Yes, perhaps Sinead would commit herself to the next 10 years.

Or maybe you're thinking of something else. Perhaps the idea is to forgo the telethon altogether and sacrifice the $80 million. The Muscular Dystrophy Assn., in its poverty, could take comfort in the thought that the pity quotient had not been exceeded.

A few less wheelchairs, a little less research, what the hey. At least Jerry Lewis would be gone, the embarrassment finally ended, the unbearable pity thing banished forever.

Where did that genuine pity begin? I am really not sure, but I do know that Jerry said yes to Paul Cohen, a friend of Jack Keller's. Paul had been dystrophic since childhood, and had dedicated himself to making the then-little-known disease more visible. He had searched for funds needed to help researchers and doctors find a cure. No one knew better than Paul the effects on patients and parents, and the dreaded financial, and physical toll. Paul Cohen had drive, but he needed the Lewis overdrive. They met. They clicked.

Jerry always did his homework. He listened to the need and then started talking with specialists. He soon discovered what muscular dystrophy was all about. He heard the professionals talk about an invisible enemy and its consequences. Jerry says he hated what he heard, but was touched by the possibility of helping. Together, he and Paul Cohen teamed up with others, and a plan to raise public awareness blossomed.

When Jerry returned from that trip to New York he told me about Paul, and the people and doctors he had met, and their work to bring hope and a cure. I asked what was needed and how we could help. His answer was almost staccato. "God knows... money and time... oh, throw in some luck!" Then he added words to the effect of, "Guess we don't take having healthy kids for granted anymore." In an almost unrelated sentence, he then attempted to describe the disease and its effects.

Neither of us spoke for a while. I was still in thought about our own boys and future children who might come into our lives. Jerry buried his head.

The silence soon translated into ideas, and a sixteen-hour fund-raising effort in New York was conceived. I recall how apprehensive he was with the unfamiliar telethon concept, wondering how it would work on radio and television. There were lots of questions that couldn't be answered until the first "ON THE AIR" sign in a small studio setting was darkened.

It did not take sixteen more hours to know. When the studio light went out, Jerry's head was already illuminated with plans for next year, the next, and the next. Some have tried to shoot that light out, but it still shines.

In the earlier days, we as a family were excited about being able to assist. One of the boys passed a coffee can in the neighborhood for "Jerry's kids." The others made their private decisions about contributions. Life was a round of endless rehearsals for Jerry. In between, he called his friends to enlist their participation. He gave it his all.

The 1965 show in Las Vegas was the first major production. At the downbeat, the boys and I were in the front row, our designated place for many years. Jerry kept our pictures in his pocket for good luck. I was often the recipient of a knowing look from him that spoke more than words. "You're there... my support... thanks."

At those telethons I made friends I have kept through the years. Like my sons, so much touches me on the inside. Robert Sampson is someone who stays in my heart. Bob came out in a wheelchair, as an adult, many years ago. He was a symbol of those who have risen above a handicap to enjoy a successful career. He was the first person confined to a wheelchair to become a vice president of United Airlines. His speech moved me to tears. He was honest, kind, and genuine. He once told me, "I can't look at you anymore, Patti. I see you cry and that breaks me up." After that, we both realized he always looked away when he spoke. It's a good thing, for my tears always flowed when I heard him.

The older children were fascinated with the many movie stars, by television itself, and by the treatment that was lavished on us as the event's "first family." The kids had their restless moments, but by and large, we were proud of them. They were good ambassadors for the host of the show and his wife.

When it was over, Jerry's hyperactive, sensitive mind pulled into neutral only long enough for a short vacation in Hawaii, on our boat in San Diego, or just in the backyard.

When the calendar moved into a new year and spring became summer, Jerry shifted back into high gear, anxiously concentrating on the upcoming Labor Day. And labor he did—obsessively. He constantly spent time talking with corporations, visiting doctors and hospitals, gaining support, and finding more stars willing to shine for kids in the darkness of the fact that there still was no cure. It was exhausting because MDA was not the only item on his jammed agenda. Exhausting, but exhilarating, for we all knew the effort brought greater hope.

The telethon brought us many proud moments. As the boys matured, they participated with Jerry in varying ways. Chris road-managed Jerry from 1983 to 1988, and traveled with him in that capacity. (He is very protective of MDA and the huge benefit the telethon garners.)

Chris: *I saw more while on the road with Dad than during my entire life before that. I have become the closest to my father of all my brothers, because, I think, we are the most alike, and it is very easy for me to understand him.*

Over the past eight years he has confided some very human

*examples of what makes him tick. I understand his insecurities,
which allows me to read him very well. I also understand his
stance about MDA.*

*I have worked in capacities ranging from production assistant
to associate producer on the MDA telethon every year since
1973, with the exceptions of 1980-81, when Father and Mom
had just split and I didn't go out of respect for Mom, and in
1990 due to the birth of my daughter, Morgan. (I did co-host
the local telethon at KCBA-TV in Salinas for the Central
California broadcast, however.)*

*I have become more involved in recent years, and have
coordinated fine art auctions that have raised in excess of
$100,000 to benefit MDA in the last three years. I also speak
at MDA fund-raisers and parties. My increased involvement
has been because of my love for my children, and being so
thankful that they are healthy.*

*Another reason, I think, is because I was able to observe
firsthand how dedicated my father is and how much hope and
joy he is able to bring to a child with a simple hello. Through
my travels with Dad, I observed dystrophic patients in every
city we visited all over the world. They were usually children,
who frequently dreamed of being able to actually meet Jerry
Lewis.*

*Arrival in a city is a whirl of interviews and rehearsals,
followed by lots of public relations events, and handshaking in
the dressing room. Before the show, there is usually a visit by a
local MDA family, and then it's time for the show.*

*By the time it is over, and the final visitor has left the
dressing room, it is after one in the morning. Everyone, especially
Dad, is beat. On the way out, the security guard tells Dad that
there is a dystrophic girl waiting in the theater to give him a
flower. Thoroughly exhausted, Dad nevertheless stops, goes
into the theater to receive the girl's floral offering, and stays to
pose for pictures taken by the child's mother. This may
sound like such a small thing, but a little child's smile of
delight says it all.*

*Unexpected requests, which Dad always tries to honor, occur
time after time, in addition to the grueling schedule of meetings
and visits set up weeks in advance. The pace he sets to try to*

accommodate everyone is just incredible, yet I have never seen him refuse to stop what he was doing and give his attention to a waiting child. Dad is always touched in return by the kids and the things they say to him.

Seeing such scenes repeated over and over convinced me to do anything I could to help these kids.

On the other side of the telethons, life went on. For Jerry, all of his projects were addictive. His "enterprise zones" were varied—in a limo, his creatively cluttered den, a hotel room, or wherever his typewriter, ink pens, and tape recorders resided for the moment. He was always so busy with scraps that I doubt he ever made a scrapbook.

At times I felt he was going in circles of diminishing size. Then I would be surprised that, out of the whirlwinds emerged new ideas, another routine, comedy changes, script possibilities, or a way to enrich a good cause.

Other wives of the tinsel set appeared to have husbands who were workaholics also. I never analyzed then, but now I think back and, having read books on the subject, I believe Jerry's work symptoms were precursors to his chemical addictions.

It was hard for him to relax. The kids were troublesome to him when they were just being kids. He was always under pressure to meet deadlines. He demanded total control. Even if he had more than one telephone ringing at once, he wanted to answer them all himself. Work became his god.

(One psychologist noted that work-addicted people suffer deep emptiness within and they try to stuff that emptiness with work. Workloads never diminish, and what is completed is never fast enough for the workaholic's expectations. Therefore, conflict is spawned.)

It would have been wonderful if, in some way, we could have personally filled Jerry's empty space with our love for him, and our deep pride in him. I believe his MDA determination is, in part, one way he attempts to fill those places. Unfortunately, his work addiction left its mark on the boys in differing ways.

Joseph, the youngest, remembers the telethons and his dad being forever in motion. A hole deepened in Joseph's life while Jerry was filling up the holes for his "other kids." Joseph has told me how proud he was of his dad's work for MDA, and that the annual telethon was great enjoyment. But it also meant his dad was not able to spend much time with him. It is one thing to be exposed to the stars and the cause—that makes you feel good. Time with dad makes you feel *great*.

Jerry's work crowded out Joseph's image of what a dad would be.

Joseph: *People ask what it's like to be a star's son. I am forced to consider the negative, very negative, and then respond, "It is great." That's a very generic answer. Being the son of a movie star of Dad's magnitude certainly had its ups and downs, but more often, it had its sideways. It was hard for me as a child to develop the proper image of my father. I lacked a father's discipline, his wisdom, his love.*

Advice from mother helped, but it was hard for her. She had the burden of being both parents. (So telethons have their charity side and sad side. Dad appeared to care more for other people's kids than for me.)

I am not sure how to assess the toll that the telethon has taken on our family. When it is weighed against the good done for others, I have to say that probably only eternity will tell. We all did the best we knew how at the time. Sometimes the passing of time and increased maturity bring life's good as well as its troubling events into perspective.

Jerry confirms that, for the first twenty-plus years with MDA, rarely a hurtful word hit the headlines. I always thought Jerry had been a wise choice for host. After a film career that had netted over half a billion dollars at the box office, he was a tailor-made host—leaving center stage and screen long enough to cry all the way to the bank for "his kids."

The insidious assaults began in 1974 ,when the rumors started that Jerry was getting rich from his charitable work.

They then escalated to accusations that he took money from "the kids."

I can state with certainty: No direct checks came to Jerry out of the funds earmarked for his kids.

Ron traveled and worked with Jerry in the telethons. He is qualified to answer the critics as he discusses the money issue and the man who has spent so much of himself battling the issue—his dad.

Ron: *In the ten years I worked on the MDA telethons, I functioned as a gofer, production assistant, and assistant director. Additionally, for a two-year period, I functioned as MDA's national youth chairman.*

Despite varying titles or responsibilities, when introduced, I was always "Jerry's kid." This was nothing new. All my life I was first "Jerry's kid," then myself. I always knew it was important to preserve a good image for the public. Personal interests were just that, personal. And the public was to be handled carefully.

It was necessary to reaffirm that Jerry Lewis does not accept money from MDA every time a reporter approached, every time I addressed meetings, or mixed with groups after a fund-raiser. Identification with this national appeal focused attention on Jerry in a positive way. MDA paid expenses, but people like to believe in selfish motives and enjoy denigrating the front man. It was in vogue to take potshots, even when the shots were directed at his family.

Yes, Jerry really helps with the fund-raising; he does not just show up and take credit for the effort of others. For years, the captains of industry had been approached by charities. What Jerry did was to turn the approach into a media event, drawing reporters to a time and place of his choosing. In a few circumstances, on a coast-to-coast hook-up, he would dare someone to refuse to contribute. They helped, and came to enjoy doing so. Jerry Lewis and MDA returned the favor by being there, for them, anytime... anywhere.

I don't know why he does the telethon. Perhaps it is because of the way the disease was originally viewed in earlier years: as the black death, beyond a cure, hard to pronounce, with victims who were hard to look at. Pain and suffering is at the heart of comedy and frankly, at the heart of Jerry's life. He grew up with it and lived it, and when he looked at muscular dystrophy, he saw a pain and suffering he understood.

He was determined to show everyone he could do something others said was impossible. A challenge made him glow, produced energy and dedication out of all proportion. I think someone told him he couldn't take on a no-win disease such as MD, and he has proven them wrong. The will to prove he is right gives him almost superhuman power over people. I have seen him look doctors in the eye and defy their opinion, contradict their advice, and be proven correct. He will prove you wrong if it takes him the rest of his life. No, he's not smarter, just more focused.

His effect on patients is awesome. He will not accept defeat and he forces others not to accept it either. He literally disregards feelings if they are not positive and hopeful. He forces people to view their lives differently, and eventually, most do. He is like an evangelist—violently challenging people to "get on with it!" And they do. There may be no mass cure, but there are multitudes of successes. The message is getting through.

Yes, Jerry is difficult to work for—that's just his style. I saw him lead rather than manage events. He just takes off in a direction and expects people to follow. He hates rules and fights bureaucracy. When he makes mistakes, he pushes so hard, so fast to fix them, you plain forget the mistakes. He runs over people who don't move, and it is necessary to understand that fact, even if it's difficult to accept it.

I no longer work with MDA or the telethon. Family issues could not be separated from the event. If I accepted the job out of a desire to help the organization, it would be interpreted as an affirmation of my filial duty to Jerry Lewis and as my taking sides with him against my mother on family issues.

We are all cheerleaders for Jerry's cause and the MDA.

I thrive on the positives. It is easy for me to become emotional about true stories that emerge from the telethons. I was touched by one family whose daughter died of the disease. At the funeral, her parents passed a flower container for contributions to MDA. Their unselfish act in a time of crisis validates the good work.

Then there was a lady in a tenement section of New York who made a five dollar pledge. Buoyed by the need of others, and aware of her own healthy kids, she got out on the street and started soliciting money for Jerry's kids. After a long, hot afternoon, she had collected $17.83. She wrote when she sent that along with her own five dollars that that was the most extra money she had ever seen. Who knows the final figures of her generosity? She did more than she could.

Teenagers in Van Nuys, California, sponsored a skate-a-thon at the Ice Capades Chalet. They collected more than twenty-thousand dollars! Just kids wanting to help.

I smile as I recall the grandmother, who, at nearly eighty-eight years of age, expressed her feelings while taking coins from an old, green, Kerr canning jar in her cupboard: "Never liked that Lewis man much, but shore do like what he does fur hurtin' kids."

Corporations and individuals—rich and less fortunate—found, through MDA, a cause where they could join hands and make a difference. Many people shed tears when the event ends and the final tote surpasses expectations. Another gold star for the comic; another impossible dream come true.

Comic? "I don't need other people's pain to make comedy," Jerry has said. "I have enough of my own." The statement puzzled organizers one year, but I understood. Telethon-related situations are not situation comedy. Critics have a field day and tabloids herald **JERRY'S QUITTING, BEING TOPPLED AS A FUTURE HOST**, or just rehash old stories. It is not pleasant when you try so hard.

I admire Jerry's courage to be an anchor for people who thrive on his cause. People like the firefighters with their boots extended as collection boxes across the country, and motorcyclists wheelin' and dealin' for Jerry.

If Jerry over-emphasizes MDA's imminent discovery of a cure, it is honest, wishful hoping. When that statement airs, people on their CB radios honk; cyclists wearing earphones pedal faster, digging harder to collect donations. One driver says he will continue driving for MDA until he cannot negotiate a car, and by then he will have found a replacement. When asked what he'll do for charity if a cure is found, he says he'll still collect to care for the kids who were too disease-progressed to be helped in time. His buddy yells over the throttle noise of a Harley-Davidson, "Jerry runs the greatest show of worth on Earth!" These people deserve medals and honors. I hope they see their long-desired goal of a cure fulfilled.

Amazing as it is, this is a show with no one sponsor, whose proceeds, other than production costs, go to kids. It is not as spontaneous as viewers may believe. Most of it is scripted. Most is live. Those who work on the sets are the least critical: They watch the various facets of Jerry's personality touch the nation's heart and tap its resources— resources as varied as the listings of people in any telephone book across the United States, Canada, and even further.

On Labor Day weekend, the telethon is background drama in every kind of home. It is a time of raising the consciousness level of financial need and maybe enabling a child to realize a dream of experiencing a week at an MDA camp.

Telethons are a time when I see Jerry putting on twin acts: his comic persona and his genuine self, the latter pulled out of hiding for this event only. I watch his legacy of love drop into every victim's family. Who can fault that?

There have been moments when I have told myself I hated what Jerry is doing, but I love the reason he does it. We have experienced moments of panic when he was ill off-camera, yet insisted on going back on. He always managed.

Gary performed at the 26th telethon with his band, Gary Lewis and the Playboys. He was slated for 2:30 a.m. Not a premiere time slot, but Gary did not complain. He was glad to be with his dad again, helping MDA. It was a rare opportunity for them to be together. When the band finished, Jerry came from backstage, reaching out to his son. Gary handed his guitar to a band member and allowed himself to be led to the center of the stage. There Jerry told the crowd how proud he was of his son and how grateful he is that his children are healthy. That was part of his motivation to give everything to the cause— that everyone deserves healthy kids.

Gary said a lot of the grief of the past disappeared that night. Both he and his dad felt a new freedom. His dad said those words that mean more than wealth or prestige, words that are healing: "I love you. You're number one." Pals again.

After the telethon, Gary, Scott, Anthony, and Chris had dinner together with their families. Scott said it was the high point of his trip. They shared, laughed, and reminisced. All were dead tired, but excited to be family again. They also discussed the solemn, frightening moments when, backstage during the show, their dad had had chest pains. The doctors were consulted, then agreed it was nothing to be concerned about.

Scott noted, "Times like the telethon tie us together on the inside. It is a time to put aside personal frustrations and recognize the value of life and family, and Dad's cause that is our cause, too. We were there for Dad and it felt good."

My heart was especially warmed when Scott told me he had seen my old friend Bob Sampson, who sent his warmest regards. Bob retired that year from his position at United Airlines. Something inside of me knows he will never retire from supporting Jerry's kids, of whom he is the oldest!

Chapter 8

"As a person, Jerry is a motion picture, a *perpetual motion* picture," a journalist once observed. Others describe him today as the former Pied Piper of the motion picture business. In a French newspaper, reviewing recent films, a critic stated, he is "still an heir to Charlie Chaplin's mantle." Jerry describes himself in the introduction to his book, *The Total Filmmaker* as "...an internationally acclaimed producer, director, and star."

At home, the kids had two perceptions of Jerry. One day Joseph, who was just a toddler, came racing to find me, saying, "Mama, Mama, come quick, *Jerry Lewis* is on television." Another time, he eagerly urged his dad to come watch Jerry Lewis with him. His observation was not unlike those of my other boys in varying situations—Jerry Lewis is a comedian, Jerry Lewis is a movie star, and another Jerry Lewis is Dad!

Fortunately for us as a family, untold millions of feet of film of Jerry Lewis, the movie star, and director, are sealed in celluloid, captured for all time—footage of more than forty movies made between 1949 and 1982.

In the earlier days of Jerry's movies, premieres were at a premium. Our excitement came from previewing the "rushes" at home. Catching glimpses of the film caused mixed emotions in me. I was proud of the good ones, but there was a side effect I rarely discussed. While watching the rushes, I could usually figure out what the real role of his "leading" lady was. It was never difficult to figure out which lady Jerry was enamored with in a particular film. She was the one who got the great close-ups, the most footage, and his attention. I found the experience painful.

It should not have been surprising. Jerry has always possessed a keen eye, an innate sense, and an ability—whether in comedy, acting, directing, or producing—to set his focus. Whether it was on a humorous line, a book, an idea, or a person, he would become obsessed with it for a time.

Film-making days were never easy days. Jerry was intense, and away a lot. He was rarely very happy with himself, especially when the shooting was not going well. Although he can read words and try to perform, he is an instinctive comedian, and must develop the character deep in his gut for it to be right in his eyes. When it was right, it was *right*. And the box office proved that!

He knew *The Nutty Professor*—a classic Jekyll and Hyde story, in which Professor Julius Kelp is tired of being pushed around and turns to chemistry for solutions to his problems—was a winner even as it was being filmed. Jerry was exuberant while shooting, although his moods changed when he was at home. His innate genius was evident and the film may be his best-remembered to date as he *became* the many faces of the former professor.

I also recall his great desire to go on the road for this film. His agents and advisors said it would be a success whether or not he did. As always, he did what he knew was right and embarked on a twenty-four city, cross-country tour that was a back-breaker. Jack Keller, his highly-admired and long-time associate, called the tour "Jerry Lewis' American Death March." Why would he make such an intense trek? "I owe it to my fans." And those fans responded.

I have had a fantasy for years about somehow organizing and developing a sequel to *The Nutty Professor*. It is my honest desire for Jerry to have long-time health and success. I would love to see him come out a winner again. And I'd like the joy of putting that fellow back to work and logging more hours on celluloid.

I cherish our personal celluloid—home movies. Living on Amalfi, we thought it would be fun to build a "playhouse" in the back yard. We installed a 16mm projector, a bar, and a barbecue. It was a great source of fun to plan and watch another dream come true. We viewed a lot of our own lives and many films in that playhouse. (It also was a super place to entertain.)

Instead of luaus, Jerry instigated "Jewaus," with the emphasis on Jewish rather than Hawaiian food and lots of Manichewitz wine. It was entertainment with a different twist. The filming rooms provided the media and equipment for great fun. Often our wonderful neighbors were guests. At various other times we entertained people like the Reagans, the Merv Griffins, the Jack Webbs, Shelley Winters, and the Tony Curtises. Jerry was a reluctant but humorous host.

When we lived on Amalfi, one of our home movie productions was the Lewis version of *Sunset Boulevard*, which we called *Fairfax Avenue*. The homemade cinema "starred" Janet Leigh, Tony Curtis, Dean Martin, some songwriters, Jerry, and me. We used cameo appearances by Jerry Livingston and Hal David. Even John Barrymore, Jr., had a small clip in one of these movies.

We staged our own personal premieres. At the presentation of *Fairfax Avenue*, Jerry invited directors Danny Mann and Hal Wallace. The men wore tuxedos and the women, including Shelley Winters, dressed in formal attire. We had a spotlight to usher them in. It was memorable!

Home movies were not uncommon on the Hollywood scene, but I believe Jerry developed and honed many of his skills in our playhouse on Amalfi, and in the other screening rooms. These experiences enabled him to become a director. He learned how to do everything—from the cameras to the lights, timing, rewrite, edit, and sets, and to deal with crews and people.

Through the years he shot scores of movies of our children growing up, and lots of me while I was pregnant or bringing another child home. He captured our vacations, boat trips, and everyday life. Now they have been transferred to video and it's wonderful to sit back and watch the past and ponder how all our lives have changed.

Despite his being Jewish, Jerry directed two of Oral Roberts' specials in Tulsa, Oklahoma. One was an Easter special. At that time, Jerry's cars had signs on the outside reading: "Super Jew." (Those cars also took me to church!) Because Jerry was working with Oral Roberts, the sign drew some adverse criticism. On that particular Easter Sunday, when the limo took the children and me to church, a parishioner read the sign and got angry. I felt badly. I think those critics were well-meaning but didn't realize we both were aware that Jesus is the Ultimate Jew. (In recent years the license plate of Jerry's Rolls Royce has read "STOP MD.")

One of the many incidents that come to mind was when Jerry was doing a film at Paramount and Elvis Presley was on the lot at the same time. One day, Elvis walked into Jerry's dressing room to say hello. Jerry was wearing one of his beautiful tuxedo shirts and Elvis expressed his admiration for it and wondered where Jerry had gotten it. After supplying the tailor's name, Jerry removed the shirt and exchanged it for the one Elvis was wearing. He came home in Elvis' plain, ordinary shirt, which bore no marking or name. I told the boys, but at that time, nobody seemed to care. For months it hung in the closet until I finally donated it to a fund-raising sale. Later I wondered who unknowingly owned a shirt that had once belonged to Elvis.

It was also at Paramount that Jerry met Barbara Stanwyck, who was doing a film on the lot. He came home saying what a gracious lady she was. A few evenings later we received a call from Barbara asking what we were doing. Jerry answered that we were watching television. She invited us over, just the way we were—Jerry, less than casual, and I, wearing one of my comfortable poodle skirts.

When we arrived, Van Johnson opened the door. Inside we were greeted by Van's wife, by Robert Stack, and by Barbara, who hugged me and took me into the bar to say hello to Robert Taylor, who was her husband at the time.

Barbara said to him, "Honey, I would like you to meet someone who can give her husband what I can't give you."

This strange introduction puzzled both Jerry and me. Then she said, "Children."

I have thought of that often. Barbara was such a lovely person. Everyone we knew loved her for her kindness and comfortable hospitality. She was a *real* lady.

Chris, Anthony, Joseph, and I went to see Jerry when he was filming *Hardly Working* in Florida. He appeared to be in a world of his own—tolerating us to some degree but never spending time with us. It bothered me, mostly for the boys. I knew he had his current girlfriend there and a lot of things were happening. He was still on Norodan, Percodan, and Valium. (It has always grieved me that the presence of his own son—Scotty—who was working with him on the film, did not deter him from conducting an affair with the woman he is married to now.)

Others from the set rounded us all up on a Sunday afternoon and took us from Ft. Lauderdale to a condo in Miami to get us out of the way. The condo was on a golf course. Jerry was seated in a comfortable chair dozing. Joseph was begging him to play golf. Jerry refused. Joseph's disappointment was written all over his face. It remains today. I tried to talk with Jerry during this time because I was so discouraged and heavy-hearted. Jerry did try to be nice and make me feel better. Shades of the past thirty-six years!

Few know the heartbreak behind the celluloid.

We always referred to the completion of a picture as delivering a baby. When the "baby" came, depression followed, because a void is left after having worked so long on a project. In fact, it was in *Who's Minding the Store?* where Jerry played Norman, that he made a provocative statement, "Women are to stay at home and have babies. Man is king in his ranch-style house." Jerry often acted as king. In retrospect, although we never lived in that "ranch-style tract house," I certainly never felt like a queen.

Hardly Working received many uncomfortable reviews. It was Jerry's first film after more than a ten-year absence. A 20th Century-Fox pickup, it was plagued with bad press and financial difficulties. Its saving face was a French one. The French have always loved Jerry and call him their Number One Buffo. A sign in front of the box office on the Champs Elysées simply reads "Jerry." It's a good summation of the cordiality between Jerry and the French public.

If I had been writing a film during these years, I may have called it *Hardly Bearable*. Jerry filed, that year, for reorganization under personal bankruptcy laws, and I filed for legal separation. For both of us, it was a comedy of terrors—a far cry from the dedication in *The Total Filmmaker:*

"To My Lady: Patti
Whose love, patience and wisdom never diminished
While waiting for me to grow up."

Reading that today, it seems a bit ironic and sardonic, but I am convinced that when he wrote it, it came from his heart—a heart that wanted to be a writer maybe more than a clown. I have so many recollections of Jerry at the typewriter, poring over words meant more for a book or a film than an audience in a Comedy Store.

Jerry kept vast amounts of notes scattered like leaves around our house. I never counted his tape recorders, but his propensity for gadgets was never satisfied. Writer Merrill Shindler observed: "The effect (of Jerry's equipment) is sort of maniacal, like a merger between Zody's and Tiffany's—which is, in many ways, a suitable metaphor for Jerry Lewis himself."

Not much has changed when it comes to more definitions or amended opinions and reviews. On the films, it started with *The New York Times* critic, Bosley Crowther, reviewing Jerry's first film, *My Friend Irma*. He wrote: "We could go along with the laughs that were fetched by a new male comedian, Jerry Lewis by name. This freakishly built and acting young man... has a genuine comedic quality. The swift eccentricity of his movements, the harrowing features of his face, and the squeak of his vocal protestations, which are many and frequent, have flair. His idiocy constitutes a burlesque of an idiot, which is something else again."

It is well-said that genius does what it must and talent does what it can. As a wife, fan, critic, and observer for more than four decades, I believe Jerry has an indefinable, toxic mix of genius and talent. His very life imitates his art. He is at home on both sides of the camera. (I am grateful to number three son, Scott, for the list of Jerry's films compiled for Appendix III. Scott worked with his dad on the sets of various films. He is gifted himself in this area. He brings to the list some of his personal thoughts and observations.

As I reread the paragraphs on Jerry's many films, well-worn memories are triggered and new ones conjured up. In the deepest sense I wonder what those films cost in the absence of a father and husband, and how that contrasts to the laughs and humor afforded to millions. I find no way to balance the two, but if pain or humor is the choice, I will opt for humor.

Scotty's list may send you back to the video store archives to decide for yourself what Jerry does best: act, direct, write, produce. Some of the above or none of the above.

Films have probably been Jerry's "high" in life. I recall his thrill over the annual stockholders' meeting of Paramount in 1965. A paragraph in that report pleased Jerry so much. After lauding some of Paramount's victories and productions, the rising tide of talent was discussed. It read:

"In this we have been aided by many outstanding producers, including in alphabetical order, Henry Hathaway, Howard Hawks, Joseph E. Levine, Edward Lewis, Jerry Lewis, Otto Preminger, Martin Ritt, Harry Saltzman, Ray Stark and Hal Wallis."

That summer, *Boeing, Boeing,* starring Tony Curtis and Jerry, was released. And the stockholders were told:

"...speaking of Jerry Lewis, we will release this summer, *The Family Jewels*, another rib-tickling comedy in the long succession of family fare from this unparalleled entertainer."

Those reports led Jerry into moving from the clown to the film teacher. A "high" came again when he was asked to conduct a post-graduate class in cinema at USC. The workshop would not be in a school room, but on various locations in keeping with "Professor" Lewis' work of the moment.

The class went very well, and other schools invited him to address their students. When he did, he encouraged young people to get involved in the industry. He stressed the importance of total commitment, responsibility, and obligation, and the heavy burden film-making demands. One student confided, "This prof is no comic. He's anathema to the image which the public has of him. My most intense prof to date!"

That should not be surprising, since Jerry was "the total film-maker."

Chapter 9

When you live in a fishbowl, there are few secrets that can be kept, although I really tried to keep tight security around our difficulties. But our own difficulties were not all we had to worry about. For many years Jerry had watchful eyes always on the boys, with security surrounding us at home and when we traveled. When I brought Joseph home from the hospital, the headlines rumored he was going to be kidnapped, so Jerry took more precautions than ever before—posting guards at the door of the hospital nursery twenty-four hours a day. (I was aware of their presence, but not told of the threats until much later.)

I was simple enough to wish for a giant Band-aid to place over the hurts of Jerry and my boys. I held onto the premise that time is the ultimate healer. And, as each new evidence of Jerry's unfaithfulness surfaced, I became more distanced from reality. I tried to shrug away the facts, believing he would change. We had dreamed of the time after the boys were married, when we would have the pleasure of being grandparents together. Then Jerry would have time to spend with our second generation. He would have every reason to be "the kid" again.

If depression is a reaction to disappointment, I should have been chronically depressed. I was not. I continued to practice a desire from my youth—to stay positive and allow my positive thinking to translate into positive living; to be optimistic and take the bitter with the better.

Then one day the stresses caught up with me and I became very ill, with severe pain. Jerry agreed to take me to the hospital, where I immediately underwent intensive testing. That night, Jerry came by in a rush. He handed me a crucifix, and said he had to dash off to Paris since he had promised Hal Wallis he would do a film there. They had shaken hands on a deal, and Jerry would never break a handshake promise. So saying, he disappeared into the night, and I dissolved into tears. The deepest pain came from his lack of concern, his not bothering to stay for the results of the tests. In time, I was diagnosed with a serious adrenal malfunction.

It was becoming more apparent that I no longer had any security to hold onto, and no category in which I could file my long-term marriage grievances. For years, I had been trying to hang on to a marriage that had ceased to possess mutuality. I was torn between the two contradictory choices: to hang on, or to let go.

My trusted advisors recommended holding on. I was encouraged to learn the art of compromise. (If compromise is an art, I have been enrolled in that school for most of my life!) Jerry's school was the school of comedy. My school was taking the brunt of his personal tragedy. In comedy, the comedian does his act and gets an immediate reaction. With the word of our impending separation and possible divorce spreading, I experienced cold reactions from many in the outer circle of our friends.

I read articles in which critics said of me, "She should have dyed her hair long ago." (They were unaware that Jerry would not allow me to do so.) I was advised, "Get out, have an affair of your own, and Jerry will be back. He's jealously possessive of you." (I couldn't.) I was told, "Hit the discos, the nightclubs. Start spreading your knowledge of what he's doing to you." (Again, I couldn't.)

At times I compared what I was going through with the times when our children had been infants and would awaken, crying, because they were hungry. Now I resembled them. I would go through months of sleeping like a baby, only to wake up crying—not for food, but for the nourishment to face one more day, one more blow, and to make the decisions that I had been purposely ignoring.

How does one still the personal eddies of loneliness, private torments, and pent-up emotions? Who would believe what I had experienced within the so-called bonds of marriage? I had been accepting of my children's divorces, but for me, right and wrong were now being reversed. I felt betrayed and bewildered.

Then a new day would dawn and I would be motivated by Dr. Robert Schuller's saying,

"Tough times never last

But tough people do.

Springtime has never failed us yet!"

My courage renewed, I would be determined to press on.

I think of my marriage to Jerry as life on the *other* side of comedy. I will never look on our thirty-six years as a journey of failure, but as one that has helped me discover the capacity to find joy and meaning in the present. A friend said to me when we were sharing our pending separations, "What a pity you gave him thirty-six years of the best years of your life." She was right, but I reminded her that Jerry had also given me thirty-six of the best years of his life. And best of all, together, we had six reasons to be forever blessed—our children.

Up until a few years before our divorce, I had been called Jerry's strength, the replenisher of his weariness. Our marriage was touted as one of the enduring ones in Hollywood, right along with those of Bob and Dolores Hope, and Danny and RoseMarie Thomas. Between us was the dream of what would happen when our sons were gone and Jerry "grew up." Those discussions started right after Dean and Jerry broke up, and were not uncommon. I kept reassuring myself that time, maturity, and faith would combine to bring us the love, security, and happy retirement we had envisioned.

I had tried to be a composite of Patti Palmer the entertainer; Esther the mother and caretaker; and Jerry's grandmother, Sarah, who had nurtured him when his parents could not. I assumed the responsibility for the boys and our home. I was lover, nurse, and friend, fulfiller of Jerry's wishes and, often, the bridge over troubled waters.

Then one day the bridge collapsed, and I became a very real actor in a living drama. I was out shopping in a supermarket, where the clerks and management were friends of mine, when I noticed a scurrying around at the checkout stands. I saw the tabloids being removed or turned over. I was curious. Then I saw the reason—these caring people were desperately attempting to shield me from a headline:

AFTER 36 YEARS I NEED TO GET OUT AND PLAY
Jerry Lewis: Why I Dumped My Wife

Just as Jerry has never forgotten the stabbing pain he experienced in his back after he fell in his Vegas act in 1965, I will never forget the excruciating stab in my heart that I experienced that day at the supermarket! I stood as if I had been freeze-dried in a very public place. Then, in a moment, I felt relief. I was glad... hurt... glad. There was nothing to hide any more.

That evening I went to church. Everyone thought I'd be devastated. I wasn't. I remember telling my friends, "Because He lives, I can face tomorrow." I had a deep sense of peace.

Ironically, I again tried to defend Jerry, as I had before. His recent years had been difficult—his father had passed away; our son had been hit by a car; and bankruptcy, real or contrived, was at his door. Jerry had never faced compound traumas well, and I had not been raised to take risks. For most of my life I had just reacted to what came along.

In all the publicity that surrounded our split, I was rarely asked my side of the story. Often, my "account" of the events was ignored or fabricated. That is the reason this book came into being.

The years of transition came at a time when I was learning to lift my eyes beyond myself, past my problems, into the limitless expanse of God's love and care. I found that God's center is everywhere, while his circumference is nowhere. I became encircled in His everlasting love.

I have often been asked what proved to be the ultimate cause of filing for separation, after so many years of my accepting Jerry's charades, his never-ending extravagances, and his lack of accountability. My response was that I had had a lifetime of little injuries before the final straw.

Friends remember Jerry as being ultra-possessive of me in the early days of our marriage. As the children came along, they saw him as jealous of the time I committed to them. But just when I would start to agree with my friends, I would get a loving note from Jerry about how much he cared for me and the pride he had in my being a good mother. These mixed messages had kept me from separating from Jerry long before we met in court.

But now Jerry was blatantly waltzing a girlfriend around the world. I'd lived through his various affairs and quick infatuations, but this was just too much! Too much for me, and way too much for our sons. Their father was not being much of an example of morality or responsibility.

I had survived the preceding few years with extremely limited income from Jerry's office. Our massive house was falling into disrepair. In fact, the boys often wondered if the house would withstand a good hard wind! We knew that Jerry was not poor. His residuals are good and ongoing. I was also aware that he was lavishing gifts on friends and spending astronomical sums flying friends around the country to join him on vacations.

I had three sons, one underage, still at home, but the days when I had had a full complement of staff—including nannies, a cook, maid, chauffeur, and gardeners—were long gone.

Jerry's reasons for separation reached me through agents and publicists, as well as through those unreliable "newspapers" that enquiring minds are eager to digest. One of Jerry's oft-repeated statements was, "Patti is one of the greatest ladies who ever lived, and I am not the best thing in the world for her anymore because my business, my work, my creativity, started to get in the way of what we had... one day I decided I had had no childhood... I really think I need to break out and play, to get some toys and play—my head needs it."

What Jerry's "head" needed had not changed much. He had always purchased his fill of toys and played to his heart's content. Our home was often referred to as his playground.

But his talk of wanting toys did not surprise me. Jerry remains a fragile, talented child-man. Most of his comedy is childlike, and he still clings to the yesterdays because he is reluctant to give up his youth!

For that reason, he abdicated much of his business affairs to incompetents. Neither of us really knew much of what went on. Unfortunately, when it came to our separation and legal encounters, I continued to believe and trust his word that he would do what was right. Foolishly, I had signed whatever he gave me through the years, for it was usually preceded by some song and dance about his just needing my signature and asking if I trusted him. Once in court a judge asked me if I knew I was being stonewalled. I was so naive, I did not even know what "stonewalled" meant. (At that time Jerry was taking out a loan on our house for drugs.)

My Catholic faith made the thought of a divorce distressing. Yet as time went on, I knew Jerry would someday have to legitimize one of his relationships. I also knew that I had walked in my husband's shadow for too long. It was time for me to step out into the sunshine, and I was determined not to act the part of a martyr. I believe there is life after divorce. I try to be a good example to my children and I have tried to be honest with each one. Jerry tried to be a husband and father, but had never had a real example to follow, so he did what he does best—he faked it, for the most part. I pressed him to spend time with the boys, to take them with him on trips, not just as paid employees of his production or film company or MDA, but as a father to his sons. With our older boys, the father-son relationships of their maturing years seemed more commercial and social. With the younger ones, it was nearly non-existent.

One of my questions of Jerry remains unanswered. How does he feel about his sons? How does he reconcile knowing so little about each one and his family? It seems they were more toys to him than people—to be played with when young, and then put aside. When they grew up, Jerry just could not handle the competition. Jerry was home only one week during our last year in Bel Air.

The boys responded in varying degrees of frustration to our marriage ending.

Scott: *My folks' divorce has to rank as my saddest recollection of my dad. For the first time he treated me and the rest of his family differently. My brothers and I had to choose sides and try to deal with the stress. I did what I could to try to help my mom.*

I lived at home with Mom and Joe after the divorce, in what seemed an incredibly cavernous house. I felt like the master of all I surveyed. Mom was taking tranquilizers and was overcome with stress. Through my faith in God I made it through. I searched my soul and knew I had to come through for my mom. And we did!

Chris distanced himself from the anguish of those trying days.

Chris: *In 1980, my parents split and I told my dad what I thought of him. Then, In December of 1982, I woke up one morning and told my wife that I thought something was wrong with my father. On the six o'clock news that night I learned he had been taken to the hospital with heart problems. I got through to him at ten the next morning. After his surgery, I was in shock. We became very close from that point on. He came down to earth and became a person to me for the first time ever. It was a very important turning point in our relationship.*

Anthony tells how the separation and divorce affected him.

Anthony: *Sometime during 1980, it was rather obvious to all of us boys, with the possible exception of Joseph, that the split was imminent. Our parents had not been together for months and seemed to be almost avoiding any kind of contact* *with one another. Naturally we spoke to people who were somewhat in touch with the grapevine and certain of their comments fortified our supposition.*

I certainly felt badly for both of my parents for many reasons—what they had shared together for those years, what they had built together, and what was to come of everything. Those are life's tragedies.

Again, the unfriendly and uninformed "rag" sheets reported my massive suit against Jerry. When I filed for a legal separation in Los Angeles County Superior Court, the alleged reasons were as off-target as the alleged reasons behind Dean and Jerry's breakup had been. And the proposed settlements were blown way out of proportion. If I had received half of some of the mentioned sums, I would be rich. I am not. Like many "grey" divorcees, I had never been schooled in the art of settlements.

(I have since been able to help many others through a group of women, who, like me, had an abhorrence for divorce, but discovered there was no choice.)

When the ultimate decision was made in court, again I was the at the mercy of attorneys. Many who observed the final proceedings related that the judge was very partial to Jerry. He gave him the most attention and showed him compassion. I was treated like the "other woman" rather than *the* woman of thirty-six years.

Our final session in the chambers moved slowly. I looked at my watch and said, "I have to hurry. I'm going to be on a television show shortly." Jerry looked aghast. Me, on a television show!

The papers were signed and just like that, a thirty-six-year marriage was dissolved, and would soon be treated as if it had never existed.

I rushed to the TV studio.

An aide of Jerry's later told me that, as he drove Jerry away from court, Jerry was fiddling with the TV dial in the back of his limo, trying to see if I really was going to appear on camera.

It was sometime later Jerry complimented me on the

appearance. I was surprised. He said I handled myself well. If I did, it was a miracle. I was so anesthetized from the proceedings, I could only do my best.

It has been said there are no friendships like those made in combat and post-divorce. I am hoping most of my readers will only have to take my word for it. At a time when one feels like an extinguished candle, you need light beyond yourself, and one candle lights another, without losing its own light. I became part of a wonderful group of other candles who had also been branded by headlines; a group of Hollywood ex-wives whose husbands had been rich and powerful, and then one day had asked for their freedom.

L.A.D.I.E.S., an acronym for Life After Divorce Is Eventually Sane, came into being at a crucial time for me. Although, like many of the others, I had a healthy dose of skepticism that anything would help, I was willing to try.

This was a time when I was forced to fasten my emotional seat belt and ride out the storm. I knew I could not do it alone. I didn't want to clothe myself with negative particles of personality. I did not want to be antagonistic. I wanted to redefine my pain and shift my focus. These women, my friends, and church helped me see beyond the moment to the possibility of a new future.

God had already proved himself to be "the keeper of my tears." I had made the decision to place myself in his unshakable security.

Woody Allen once quipped that "marriage is the death of hope." I am not sure how he defines divorce. Yet through divorce I learned what hope is all about. I learned to accept the fact that when God brought me to a crossroad, it is his business to take me beyond my broken heart and fractured dreams. I learned the true meaning of friendship... with God and the L.A.D.I.E.S. as my forever friends.

The L.A.D.I.E.S. organization, formed about 1982, was comprised of a nucleus of women who had been married to men in the entertainment field and whose divorces occurred in later life. Some of those involved during my readjusting years were former wives of men like Michael Landon, Flip Wilson, George Segal, Ken Berry, Glen Campbell, Leonard Nimoy, Eric Estrada, Don Knotts, Buddy Ebsen, Gavin MacLeod, and Pat Morita. Most of us would be seeing our former husbands on television, in the movies, and on marquees throughout the rest of their lives. Most of us were mothers. Many were recipients of their husband's high-priced lawyer's perception of alimony, which usually proved insufficient.

As we came to peace with ourselves and trusted each other, we reached out to other women who needed advice and counsel. We compiled lists of the attorneys who are most attentive to women's support needs, of organizations that could help, and of psychologists and counselors who had proved competent and understanding.

Then, in 1991, I was asked by the Christian Broadcasting Network in Virginia Beach, Virginia, to speak at the opening of their Founder's Inn. During the event, I met hundreds of women who had been jettisoned after several decades of marriage into a world of which they were ill-prepared, psychologically, and financially.

There I gained a confidence and freedom to give myself and my experiences away. To turn hurt into help is an important key to the healing process. They asked a lot of questions about L.A.D.I.E.S., and about me personally, and they shared their own heartbreaks.

I told them that our group meets once a month at each other's homes, where we talk about the various stages we are in during our divorce process. When a new "girl" (under fifty) comes in, she often just cries through the meeting. We affirm and encourage her, assuring her that she will survive.

I have found from experience that recovery takes longer for some than for others. With the divorce rate in America running about one million a year—the highest in the Western World—it isn't surprising so many are left floundering. The hoped-for, *On Golden Pond* years disappeared with the marriage.

One thing I impressed on the women at CBN was to

get together with trusted people, but to avoid husband-bashing, which only makes people ugly. The anger that fuels it shows on a woman's face and it may alienate the children, many of whom are still hoping for reconciliation, and missing their fathers. I know that was true for my sons. Usually the children think that when dad divorced mom, he divorced them, too. We need to reassure them they are loved by both.

When one of the group has to appear in court, I told the people at Founder's Inn, another in the L.A.D.I.E.S. organization accompanies her to offer support and prayer. One of our recurring lines when someone is in trouble is, "Did you know you were going to grow up to be in a group with all these wives of famous men?" We all laugh knowingly at that. Rarely do we discuss our husbands as our "ex" or "ex-husband." All of us are displaced homemakers. Through L.A.D.I.E.S., the organization called Displaced Homemakers gained new visibility and is active in many cities across America. Its members are a reservoir of knowledge compiled from experience.

I shared with the ladies at Founder's Inn how I personally went through a time of intense hurt, which changed to anger, and then finally to acceptance. It is not easy to get on with your life after a divorce, and at times I felt scared to death. But I realized I had only died to myself. The time had finally come when I said, "I'm not going to take this anymore. I am going to do some constructive things. I am going to put this whole mixed-up mess in God's hands and let Him work it out." He did!

There was a period when I shunned going to church. I think I was trying to punish God—as if I could! I thought the divorce was His fault. One day I said to my priest, Father Elwood Keiser, "Father, all these things happening to me are unfair and unjust."

He replied, "Look at it this way, Patti. You are going through purgatory on Earth, and when you die, you'll go straight to heaven." He also reminded me of the need to become re-involved in church and I chose to rejoin St. Paul the Apostle's sanctuary choir. I became the music librarian, and met wonderful people. As we sang the psalms, anthems, and scripture, tears flowed down my face. Music became a great release for me again. The congregation accepted me as a person, not a personality. Our choirmaster, Dr. Jon Wattenbarger, became like another son. When Jon learned I was writing a book, he wanted to be a part. Like some of my other friends, he was overly generous with his comments:

"Patti Lewis stands out as one of the truly unique people ever to become part of my life. Her uniqueness lies in the fact that Patti keeps things simple. Her characteristics are well-defined. She has a consistent personality which, while it grows through the years, remains identifiable and dependable.

"Patti's trials seem to have been like Isaiah's, "refiner's fire." They have only served to polish a personality that is as strong as a diamond and as sparkling with quality as a precious jewel. To dwell on these qualities would be to say that Patti is a woman of deep faith in herself and in the people she loves. She places trust in these folks, and when she is let down by them, she forgives and is patient. She does not withdraw her faith in the people she has chosen to befriend. Patti is a friend's friend. She is loyal in the truest sense, which is to say she is totally honest with her friends. She speaks truth and maintains confidences. Patti is the soul of discretion, but never fails to give wise counsel when she sees fit."

When our L.A.D.I.E.S. group was the subject of a story in *McCalls* magazine, we were suddenly inundated with mail from all over the world. A man who had a dude ranch in Australia sent a picture. He wanted "the girls" to visit him. Another gentleman sent a picture of himself with a proposal of marriage for one of the girls—it didn't matter which one!!

One man suggested that our husbands form a group and call it G.E.N.T.S.—God Eventually Nails The Suckers.

Dr. Robert Schuller invited me to speak on his "Hour

of Power" telecast. I shared with his audience the story of a lady who had written me saying she was so morose she wanted to kill herself, since she couldn't live without her husband. I wrote back, "What a wonderful idea. Now you will alleviate your husband's expense for attorneys. He will get the kids, the car, the house, and everything!" My letter shocked her and woke her up. Now she is doing fine.

The best way to triumph over disappointment is to talk about it with real friends. I am blessed with many. Through the years I've had Lori Caldwell as confidante and understanding friend. To have people you can trust is a treasure. Listen to their advice. Sometimes I didn't, and was sorry later.

The women in the audience laughed as I told them about the time I was with Jerry at Dodger Stadium. He had been playing ball with the team. A little kid came up to me and asked, "Lady, are you Jerry Lewis' mother?" I said, "Yes, I am. Where would we be without mothers!"

The women understood that answer. We all have to raise our husbands to some degree.

In the L.A.D.I.E.S. group we share a common denominator. We all married the same man! It's true! Those who practice therapy in the screen colony explain that many of the men suffered rejection in their youth and have grown up to be difficult husbands. Those in our group—and probably those in the audience—unanimously agreed. Research shows that entertainers and, more specifically, comedians, have the most trouble adjusting to marriage. Their sensitivity and insecurity compounds their fear-ridden personalities.

I was asked—as I often am—if I have forgiven Jerry. The answer is yes! And I felt such freedom when I did; freedom from the perpetual motion, the treadmill, and the excessive responsibility of trying to hold our lives together. Even more importantly, I forgave his unfaithfulness and his philandering ways. That was the toughest. But Jesus reminds us that we must forgive to be forgiven. I've learned that forgiveness is a gift and a sacrifice I can give back to the Lord, expecting nothing in return except his warm approval. That is the best kind of gift. I carry no malice. I try to multiply my good memories and keep them from becoming brittle.

During the Christmas holidays in 1981, just before Jerry was to come for his personal belongings, the "Bing Crosby Holiday Special" was on. Under the touching seasonal music, Bing was narrating the story of Jesus. I cried, then picked up my Bible to seek comfort. Jerry would be arriving shortly. I opened God's book to Proverbs 28:1, "The wicked flee when no man pursues them, but the righteous are bold as a lion." That was my message from God. I was making no condemnation or correlation. But for some reason, I felt settled.

I closed the seminar in Virginia with the story of meeting with a number of senators' wives in Washington, D.C. I knew none of the ladies there. But at the end, a woman in a wheelchair came toward me and softly stated, "You know Jesus, don't you?" She paused and finished, "It shows in your face." That was the ultimate compliment. I want the beauty of Jesus to shine through me and encourage others.

There is a saying that sums up my philosophy about this. I don't know who wrote it, but it's true and motivates my life.

"At twenty, you have the face you inherited.

At forty, the face you developed.

At sixty, the face you deserve.

All the good times and good deeds are written there. You have come to a diamond point of brilliance with your beauty that should be shared. It goes with a sense of judgment and life experience. It's a time to teach—as well as to learn even more. This is when you should stand the tallest, literally, and figuratively. It is perhaps the most individual period for your looks and physical bearing. You can project: 'Here I am. This is what I've done. I wouldn't change any of it. And there's more— much more to come.'"

Appendix I

I had felt unprepared for life when I married, so I wanted my boys to grow up as whole people. After all, they might have to face obstacles as Jerry and I had—and they might not always be surrounded by maids and staff to meet their whims and fancies.

So I decided that each of the boys should learn to cook. Although I did not agree with Mama's forcing me to be adept at "what all good little girls must learn," I had lived long enough to know that cooking was essential to living, even for "good little boys."

It has been said that:
We may live without poetry, music and art;
We may live without conscience, and live without heart;
We may live without friends; we may live without books;
But civilized man cannot live without cooks!

—Edward Robert Lytton, 1860

The old adage that "boys will be boys" was never more evident than in our kitchen. Climbing, crawling, mixing, matching, measuring—they were always stirring up something, and frequently much more than just batter.

I smile as I look back, wondering if I was not the original "batter'd" woman, and those little chefs "flour" children before their time! Their little pink cheeks would be dusted with flour, and sugar would be spilled and scattered like snow on my countertops, which the youngest ones were barely able to reach. In their childish imaginations they shared the fantasy that the sugar was fresh-fallen snow, and they created a wonderful winter road for their fleet of toy cars and trucks.

What fun to see again through their eyes and observe their innocent make-believe.

The agile little fingers that colored and decorated eggs at Easter generally had difficulty landing them within the confines of a mixing bowl. Usually by the time the contents of the recipe went into the oven, I had another afternoon's work to clean up my dirty half-dozen!

In the kitchen we learned a lot together—about life and recipes for living. One of my yellow, egg-stained favorites was called, "Recipe for a Home."

One-half cup of friendship;
Add one cup of thoughtfulness.
Cream together with a pinch of powdered tenderness.
Beat very lightly in a bowl of loyalty.
Add the vital ingredient of faith,
One cup of hope and a generous cup of love.
(Some days double the love and faith—a mother's secret
    for a well-raised, finished product.)
Be sure to add a spoonful of gaiety that sings,
With the ability to laugh at little things
And overlook the non-essential items.
Moisten with the sudden tears of heartfelt sympathy.
Bake in a good-natured pan and serve repeatedly.

In the kitchen I could practice my own version of "show and tell." It was a perfect place to impress on their minds that not just their mom and dad, but everyone they would meet knows something they don't know, but need to learn. Every person and experience is a potential learning source. From cakes that fell due to the children's impatience to wait for the needed cooking time, to cookies that burned because of inattention, they learned what I repeat so often, that no failure is final.

In more ways than one, life, real life poured out of the mixing bowl.

I may not agree with all the philosophies of a century ago, but the last line is correct: cooking is essential.

I wanted the boys to learn to cook in a way that would make it seem fun, rather than difficult. I wanted it to be something productive and meaningful for their future that we could do together.

I am amused at their recollections of these times, and not unaware that it meant more to some of them than the others. Still, all six know their way around the kitchen.

One of my friends used to say to me, "Don't bury yourself in the business of raising your children instead of facing a problem with your husband." In retrospect, I realize I did just that. I buried myself in the lives of the children and hoped my problems with Jerry would resolve themselves. Occasionally they did, but more often they did not.

When it came to cooking choices, Scotty favored Italian cookies called "Farfoletti." He reminded me that "you always let us participate when you cooked. Either we'd knead dough or help prepare the ground beef for meatballs. Sometimes we watched and wondered if those little round balls would substitute for basketballs or pinballs. Could we shoot them like bowling balls across the floor? Sometimes you made those Italian cookies. We all loved watching and getting involved."

While Anthony was another farfoletti fan, he also shared my love of the garden.

Anthony: *The garden was Mother's spiritual place. Regardless of what was going on around her, she always managed to find peace working in the garden. The tranquillity was further enhanced by two near-life-sized statues—Moses at one end of the backyard and Saint Anthony at the other. (They made the move with her and now reside in Brentwood.) Being in this kind of biblical/religious company sort of does something to you.*

It is said that our creations are an extension of the soul. The garden, vibrant with the brilliant colors of a wide variety of blooms and plants, was a quietly beautiful testament to Mother's positive attitude, love of God, and appetite for life. I recall spending quite a bit of time watching her plant and nurture all her botanical "children." All of us boys developed pretty green thumbs ourselves and grew some very impressive vegetables and fruits in our own little gardens.

I sometimes wonder if the farfoletti cookies were a favorite for taste or because they ultimately progressed into the shape of butterflies. I had no trouble, however, obtaining an eager, active line-up to roll out the dough, knead it, and impatiently wait for the pastry cutter. Then came the tying of the pastry into bow-tie knots of every size and shape. Sprinkling on the powdered sugar provided the frosting on another day of cooking lessons.

Gary, being the oldest, was proficient at combining things in the kitchen. (It is no surprise that, through the years, he has organized bands and been successful with people.) He helped with the younger ones and was accurate in measuring. He helped pour the batter into the greased layer pans with a unique deftness that bespeaks the mind of the musician he is today.

Chris enjoyed most of the activities in the kitchen.

Chris: *My mom taught me the basics of cooking pasta, sauce, marinated steaks, hamburgers, chocolate cake, cookies, and farfoletti (Christmas cookies), baking, broiling, and barbecuing. We were always encouraged to make our own things. We all enjoyed being with her in the kitchen.*

I especially enjoyed one pasta sauce Mom was making when she opened a can of tomato paste that exploded, sending tomato goo into every nook and cranny of that 500-square-foot kitchen. My brothers and I laughed for years about that.

Ron was the sandwich specialist. I put aprons on all the boys to help deflect flying flour and prevent stains. What fun we had!

The children developed favorite parts of the recipe process. Ron and Chris were the cutters while Gary and Anthony were the cut-ups! Joseph, the baby, just watched, eager-eyed and wanting to mimic his brothers, while Scotty master-minded the spills. He had lots of experience playing pick-up with liquid and solids alike.

The classic Gingerbread Man held a certain fascination for my boys and they loved the story that Abraham Lincoln told of a time when he had lived in Indiana and his mother had bought ginger and sorghum to make gingerbread. (That rare occurrence was always a significant treat because their finances were so limited.) When he came home from school, Lincoln smelled the gingerbread. His mother had baked three gingerbread men, and gave Abe all three. Quietly, in his lanky, somewhat awkward gait, the future president of the United States made his way outside and settled under his favorite hickory tree. As Abe was preparing to relish his treat, a boy from an even poorer family who lived down the road arrived and sat down beside him.

"Abe," he asked, "gimme a man?"

When he received it, he crammed it into his mouth and devoured it in two bites. While young Lincoln was slowly and methodically savoring the legs of his first cookie, the boy said,

"Abe, gimme that other 'n."

He wanted it himself, but out of his kindness, Abe handed it over, thinking this kid sure liked gingerbread.

The lad remarked, "I don't s'pose anybody on earth likes gingerbread better 'n I do—and gets less 'n I do."

What a warm story of a giving heart, from one who had so little to give. Using tales like this, I often tried to teach the children to share. Assuming the responsibility of raising lifelong learners of the truth, "of those to whom much is given, much is required," was one of my goals.

Jerry and I had our favorite foods. He loved Italian Chicken and apparently still talks about Chocolate Pudding Cake. I enjoy Banana Cake and Olive Onion Bread. These, and others of my resident recipes are weathered by time and multiple use.

Today, as I flip through the cookbooks and recipe cards, I am flooded with memories of many yesterdays, yesterdays when I was surrounded by my own little celebrities.

Six boys in the kitchen were onstage (but did not know it) playing the opening acts of the rest of their lives. And their curtain calls at the end of the day were wonderful celebrations. They had great expectations and anticipation as we opened the oven and shared our "reviews." Then we sat around the table and tasted the success or discussed the failures. Together we learned that some goals are so worthy, it is glorious even to fail!

When all was said and done, one way to describe our early baking lessons was as follows:

Let Gary light the oven—he's the oldest—and get out the spoons, bowls and ingredients.

Remove Joseph's blocks and Anthony's toy autos from the kitchen table.

Let Gary measure the flour—extra to compensate for what will be spilled.

Have Ronnie help remove assorted-sized hands from the flour—every kid wants to imitate the Pillsbury dough-boy.

Wash flour off kids. Measure flour to replace flour on the floor.

Put flour, baking powder, and salt in sifter.

Line up Chris and Scotty to sift. Let Scotty pick up the spills.

Get dustpan and brush up pieces of the bowl that was just knocked on the floor. Treat gently the tears that follow.

Get another bowl.

Answer the telephone.

Return to the kitchen.

Look for the missing egg.

See what the dogs are lapping up from the floor.

Answer the doorbell.

Return.

Take out the pans.

Remove several tablespoons of salt from the pans.

Put shortening-covered matchbox toy in sink.

Start scavenger hunt to have the boys pick up the scattered nutshells, making a path all the way to the bathroom.

Wash up kids. Wash up kitchen floor. Wash up walls. Wash dishes. WARNING: Wash up all of the above only after the cooking school has been dismissed and the students have recessed to the play-yard.

Call the neighborhood bakery. Order what we intended to bake.

Make diary entry—tomorrow we will try again.

Try again we did! And again and again.

Here are a few family favorites you, too, might enjoy:

BANANA CAKE

1/2 cup butter or margarine, softened; 1-1/3 cups sugar; 2 eggs; 1-1/2 tsps. vanilla; 2 cups flour; 3/4 tsp. salt; 1 tbsp. baking powder; 1/2 cup milk; 1 cup mashed bananas (2 or 3); 1 cup sour cream; 1 12-oz. package semisweet chocolate pieces, melted

Cream butter and sugar until fluffy. Beat in eggs and vanilla. Mix flour, salt and baking powder. Beat into batter alternately with milk, ending with flour mixture. Fold in mashed banana. Turn into 2 greased and floured 8" round cake pans. Bake at 350 degrees 30 to 35 minutes, or until light touch in center leaves no imprint. Cool 10 minutes in pans. Remove from pans and cool on racks.

Blend sour cream into warm, melted chocolate. Spread over cake and stack layers. Decorate with sliced bananas just before serving, if desired.

OLIVE ONION BREAD

2 cups biscuit mix; 2 tbsp. chopped parsley; 2/3 cup cold water; 2 cups thinly sliced onions; 2 tbsps. butter; salt and pepper; 1/2 cup sour cream; 1 egg, beaten; 1 tsp. dill weed; 3/4 cup pitted California olives, sliced

Mix together biscuit mix, parsley and water; spread in greased 8"x8" pan. Sauté onions in butter until golden, season to taste with salt and pepper. Combine sour cream, egg, dill weed, onions and olives. Spoon over bread mixture. Bake at 450 degrees for 20 minutes. Cut into squares for serving.

CHOCOLATE PUDDING CAKE

Combine 1 package chocolate cake mix, 1 package (4-serving size) instant chocolate pudding mix, 4 eggs, 1/4 cup butter, 1 cup milk. Beat at medium speed 2 minutes. Add 1 cup chopped nuts and 1 cup chocolate morsels. Pour into 2 greased, floured 8" cake pans. Bake at 350 degrees for 50 minutes or until cake springs back when pressed lightly. Cool 10 minutes before removing from pans. Brush with 2 tbsp. heated honey and butter. Sprinkle top with additional nuts.

PATTI'S ITALIAN CHICKEN

Brown one 4-pound cut-up roasting chicken in 1/4 cup olive oil or shortening in heavy skillet. Remove and put in a large casserole dish. In a skillet, combine 1 cup chopped tomatoes (or a 16-oz. can) with 1/2 cup chopped onions, 1/2 cup chopped green peppers, 1 minced clove garlic, 2 whole cloves, 2 bay leaves, a pinch of oregano, 2 tsp. salt and 1/2 tsp. pepper.

Simmer 5 minutes. Pour over chicken. Brown 1 cup uncooked rice in oil. Add to chicken. Cover with water. Bake in 350-degree oven 1-1/2 hours or until chicken is tender.

To casserole, add 1/4 cup chopped pimento, 1 cup drained, cooked peas, and 1 cup of sliced ripe olives. Bake 15 minutes more. Serves 6 to 8.

FARFOLETTI DOLCI

6 eggs; 3 tbsp. granulated sugar; 3 cups flour; 1/2 tsp. orange flavoring; 1/2 cup powdered sugar; 1/4 tsp. salt; 2 tsp. butter; 1 tsp. almond flavoring; 3 cups Crisco (or more).

Beat eggs lightly. Add granulated sugar, salt, and flavorings. Blend thoroughly. Place flour on board, cut in butter, and add egg mixture. Knead until smooth ball is obtained. If dough is too soft, gradually add a little flour to make firm, but not hard. Set aside for thirty minutes, then cut dough in four sections. Roll on well-floured board until wafer-thin. Cut with pastry cutter into strips 6" long by 3/4" wide. Tie in individual bow-knots. Fry bows in deep hot oil about 3 minutes or until lightly browned. Drain on absorbent paper. Cool and sprinkle with powdered sugar. Makes about 6 to 7 dozen bow-knots.

PATTI'S VINEGAR CAKE

1/2 cup butter; 1-1/2 cups sugar; 2 eggs; 1 tsp. vanilla; 2 squares bitter chocolate, melted; 1/2 tsp. salt; 1 cup sour milk; 1 tbsp. baking soda; 1 tbsp. vinegar

Cream together butter and sugar until light and fluffy. Stir in eggs. Add vanilla and blend well. Add chocolate. Sift flour with salt and add to creamed mixture alternately with sour milk. Mix together soda and vinegar and add to mixture. Pour into 2 greased 9" cake pans. Bake at 375 degrees for 25 minutes.

Sugar cookies were a favorite for everyone except Chris. Diversity shows up in countless ways. This basic sugar cookie recipe was a holiday staple.

SUGAR COOKIES

1/2 cup butter; 1 cup sugar; 2 eggs; 1 tbsp. milk; 1 tsp. vanilla; 1 tsp. baking powder; 2 cups flour

Cream butter and sugar, beat in eggs one by one. Alternately add flour sifted with baking powder and milk and vanilla. Chill in the refrigerator for at least two hours. Roll out 1/4" thick (or slightly thicker) and cut with a large, round cutter. Sprinkle with sugar (mixed with nuts or cinnamon if you like) and bake at 375 degrees for 10 to 15 minutes. This would be an easy first step into rolled cookies. They can be formed into balls, placed on the cookie sheet, and pressed down with the bottom of a glass which has been dipped in ice water.

Variations: 1 tbsp. grated orange rind may be used instead of vanilla with orange juice substituting for milk. Grated rind can also be mixed with sugar for the topping. The same can be done with lemon rind and juice.

EASY GINGERBREAD
5 cups flour; 1-1/2 tsp. baking soda; 2 tsp. ginger; 1-1/2 tsp. cinnamon; 3/4 tsp. cloves; 1/2 tsp. allspice; 1 cup shortening; 1 cup sugar; 1 egg; 1 cup molasses; 1-1/2 tbsp. vinegar; 1/2 tsp. salt

Stir together all dry ingredients. Beat shortening and sugar until light and fluffy. Add egg, molasses, and vinegar; beat well. Add dry ingredients slowly to sugar mixture, beating well. Cover and chill at least 3 hours or overnight. Divide dough into thirds. On a lightly-floured surface roll dough to 1/4" thickness. (Keep remainder chilled.) Cut into desired shapes. Place 1-inch apart on greased cookie sheet and bake at 375 degrees for 7 or 8 minutes. Cool 1 minute, remove to wire rack. Depending on size of cookie cutter, makes 30-50 men.

Joseph, our youngest recalls some of our cooking experiences fondly.

Joseph: *I cannot remember back to the first time my mom taught me how to cook because I was so young. She let me get my little fingers into everything—from spaghetti sauce to chocolate chip cookie batter. Of course, my favorite thing to cook with Mom was her Italian food. When it came to making meatballs, we would all have our hands in the meatball-making process and lots of times we made a mess. But my mom was never angry. She only offered advice.*

Our favorite meatball activity was to make a nice round ball, then put our initials in it. We would then look for that particular one once the dish hit the table. Although we never found any surviving monograms, Mom still encouraged us to have as much fun as we could when we were cooking.

Those kitchen sessions inspired me to go on to learn more about culinary art. Mom was kind enough to send me to cooking classes at UCLA, where I learned the art of Chinese cooking from the famous chef, S.T. Ling Wong. Because of the basic knowledge Mom gave me, as well as her influence, I became proficient in cooking all types of cuisine.

Scotty wrote of his kitchen learning experiences.

Scotty: *My relationship with my mom is great. She does everything in her power to help Deby and me and we do the same for her. We get together on weekends at mom's house. Anthony, his wife, Sharon, and his two kids usually like swimming in the pool. Sometimes we barbecue. I think my mom and I understand each other better than ever. She's constantly teaching me things when I think I have learned it all.*

When I hear Scotty share that he is *still learning*, it boosts my confidence. After all, that is what moms are for—to keep loving and teaching, sharing and caring. Even today, as I sit on a high stool at a much smaller kitchen counter with another in our long line of English Springer Spaniels underfoot, I look out of the window and watch my children and their next generation joyfully laughing and splashing, I think *true wealth is what you are—not what you have.*

My wealth is measured in this special love for all my boys and their families.

Appendix II

Walking up the steps to Patti's gracious home in Brentwood, California, is like discovering a peaceful garden oasis. Flowers bloom year-round, sundials and plaques grace the landscape. Over the doorway is a wooden carving. Its message—LOVE ONE ANOTHER—epitomizes the lady who placed it there.

Entering the house is like knocking on history's door and not being disappointed. Homemade memories are mixed with a gallery of photo remembrances.

Old-world elegance meets new-world ambiance. The highlights are carefully crafted scrapbooks, pictures and portraits, worth more than a million words.

This house, a far cry from the Louis B. Mayer mansion, with its twelve bedrooms and seventeen bathrooms, is a small unique place that has become a repository for scores of years of memories.

You are invited to spend time with the curator, the lady of the house. She will bring her gallery to life, and put varying faces to people you have read about. You will meet her family, displayed on the walls in every room, and come away with a true portrait of what is important to Patti Lewis.

I still feel the excitement of a child when I realize Jerry has known nine presidents! I met many of them, and watched him perform for five. Presidents Franklin D. Roosevelt, Harry S. Truman, Dwight D. Eisenhower, John F. Kennedy, Lyndon B. Johnson, Richard M. Nixon, Gerald Ford, Jimmy Carter, Ronald Reagan: these pictures tell quite a story. Not just a story of men who worked in the Oval Office, but of their taste in humor, their place in history, and the common denominator they all shared— the need to laugh.

John F. Kennedy was a personal friend of Jerry's. They had met sometime around 1950 at a Chicago hotel, quite a while before JFK's presidency. According to Jerry, he even tucked some gags into the then-senator's speeches. Their friendship was never a press item, and his death pressed heavily on my husband.

Hubert and Muriel Humphrey were also our friends. Hubert appreciated Jerry's work with Muscular Dystrophy. Once, when we were the guests of George Meany, the union organizer, and the Humphreys were in town campaigning, they visited with us at one of the parties.

The first time I met Ronald Reagan was at the home of Marie MacDonald. We started discussing politics as soon as we were introduced. I became aware of his intense interest in the world and all people. I was amazed at his broad knowledge. On another occasion, he and Nancy invited us for dinner, and Ronnie gave me my first instruction in the wonder of a telescope. He is such a gentleman. But today I still smile when I think of a time we went to the movies with them and he was fussing with a contact lens. He carefully put it in his mouth and then replaced it in his eye. With that wonderful Reagan grin he commented, "I'm just cleaning my lens before the movie!"

When I first saw Barbara Bush at the White House, I was surprised that she quickly recalled the time we had been together at a Child Help luncheon some years earlier. She's such a gracious lady.

The Lewis family received the royal treatment on many occasions, one of which makes me smile. If I were painting the background landscape to the scene, it would be the royal blue waters that surround Monaco. In the early '70s, Jerry did a show for Prince Rainier and Princess Grace. In the box, I was introduced to the darling princesses: Stephanie, and sixteen-year-old Caroline, who confided to me that the press had her making marriage plans to Prince Charles of England. She was laughing, saying she did not even know him.

Jerry has performed for four royal families. He has met kings and queens, and if you want more, his bios probably say he also knows Dr. Jonas Salk and Dr. Michael DeBakey, (who has remained my dear friend through the years) has flown a 747, steered the Queen Elizabeth (I was there), gone underwater in submarines, flown in a F-18, and gone through a good many fortunes!

Over here is another favorite—Jimmy Durante, who was such a friend to children. He played at neighborhood parties when he was young, as I had. He and his wife Marjorie were genuine friends. They cared for everybody. Marjorie used to say—and I could certainly understand— "Jimmy represents the whole human race. He copies nobody. He's himself reincarnated into whoever he needs to be." Jimmy was a songwriter, a fact many people may not remember. If behind the mask of a clown there was a tragic individual wanting to be loved, he expressed it in his songs. Jimmy didn't have to warm up his audience. They already belonged to him while they stood in line waiting for the show, and they carried him with them into everyday life.

Dick Martin was the bartender when Dean and Jerry played at Slapsie Maxie's in Hollywood. After watching them perform, he announced he was going to be a comic, too. Years later, he became part of the Rowan and Martin team. I wonder how many others Jerry has inspired.

George Burns and Gracie Allen left a lingering legacy as husband-wife partners. George had an insightful line that could be representative of all comedians.

"If I get someone to laugh, I'm a comedian.

If I get a little laugh, I'm a humorist.

If I get no laughs, I'm a singer.

If my singing gets laughs, I'm a comedian again."

At age 95, George was offered a five-year contract at the Riviera in Las Vegas. He said he would only sign for two, but *if* the management was still around then, he'd take another five!

Another great star and entertaining lady was Loretta Young. We were invited to dinner at her place on several occasions. At one party, I was watching Tyrone Power and his wife, Linda Christian. A few minutes later, I saw Loretta take Linda into what I assumed was her bedroom. When they reappeared, Linda was wearing a large brooch she had not worn upon arrival, and the lines of her drastically low-cut neckline had been redrawn.

The seating arrangement had me, as a newcomer to town, between Tyrone, and Ricardo Montalban. Van Johnson was across the table. What an experience for Esther Calonico from Wyoming! During another visit at Loretta's we were introduced to Ingrid Bergman, who was at that time doing *Cactus Flower* with Walter Matthau.

One of the first true art galleries I visited was the home of Edward G. Robinson. Everywhere you looked in that massive house were genuine works of art. Sculptures, Picassos, many of the original works of the greats were magnificently displayed. I felt like a guest of the present and the past. The garage, too, had been converted into a gallery, and in one corner was his favorite picture of his mother. I was touched by the warmth and sentimentality of this man, who had portrayed so many tough gangsters in films. He was caring and solicitous, even insisting that I use the elevator/chair in the back of the house to go upstairs, since I was several months pregnant.

Cecil B. DeMille and Y. Frank Freeman, head of Paramount at the time, whose pictures are on this wall, remind me of when Jerry was in the hospital with a bleeding ulcer. They came to visit. What a duo! They had brought him a handful of candy bars. (It was an open secret that any director having problems with Jerry on the set could calm him, not with a pocketful of miracles, but with lots of candy bars.) Both of them tried to convince him to slow down, yet left knowing he would do as he pleased!

Speaking of candy, the original "candyman," Sammy

Davis, Jr., was a real friend. In the roles of singer, activist, actor, and cultural phenomenon, his sixty years in show business will not be forgotten. He'll be long remembered by our sons. In London, while Jerry was directing Sammy and Peter Lawford, Sammy took a special interest in the boys. He had a gift of giving himself away to kids. Ours loved him.

The son of another dancer, Sammy was the epitome of the American entertainment that evolved from vaudeville. His last days were sad days for us all, as we prayed for his recovery and the resumption of another leg of his worldwide tour with Frank Sinatra and Liza Minnelli. Just the word "Sammy" calls to mind a host of memories.

Let me suggest that, if you ever attempt to paint a picture of non-stop life, the subject who would splash the brightest colors over your canvas would be Jerry Lewis. He makes you see comedy not as an art or science that can be explained, but as one that can be experienced. His brush strokes of instinct marked each performance and picture. His formula for success can be measured only in receipts from the box office and a rarely expressed personal satisfaction. His mark was left on every house we lived in, and remains on mine today. His greatest contribution to my life was our children. You will see them in every room of my home and they are inwardly visible in every crevice of my heart.

Let's make a quick stop in the guest bathroom, where pictures hang of my kids, and their kids—in all stages of the bathing and washing process. Pictures of tender little bodies reaching for rubber ducks, splashing, smiling, posing, cover the walls. It is an unusual feature of the decor.

Patti becomes solemn and a bit distant as she moves on. There are very few pictures of Patti's mother, father, and brother Joe displayed on the wall here. They are not available. The imprints of "negatives" were developed inside. She has some good memories too, though some of them are underexposed. She tells of visiting aunts in Italy and, seeing their poverty, becoming aware of how fortunate she had been in many ways. She quickly passes the sparse display of her own childhood, casting off as unimportant her personal career, which still remains an impressive part of her resume. Others are her priority during this unique opportunity to visit a home so prolific with memorabilia.

Come through the kitchen. A lot of what is displayed here is my own handwork and some of my favorite sayings. If you'd like to step from the dining room to the patio outside for a breath of air, please do. My garden is my solace. The statutes of St. Anthony and Moses will always be significant to me.

Another favorite saying expresses my heart.

"Count your garden by the flowers
Never by the leaves that fall
Count your days by golden hours
Count your nights by stars, not shadows.
Count your life by smiles, not tears
Count your joys with children, not fears
Count your age by friends, not years."

A stunning piece of Steuben crystal graces my dining-room table. It had been on the dining table at the Mayers' when we purchased their house, and Mrs. Mayer insisted that I keep it. The marvelous handblown glass is a symbol of giving and kindness. I am reminded that sometimes the things you keep, you lose, and the things you give away, you keep forever.

Our living room is covered, for the most part, with photo-furnishings of family. I see the boys in every pose and circumstance—clowning, posing, being boys, growing, maturing, with and without their dad. The foremost reason for lining the walls with these nostalgic reminders is so I will never lose sight of those I love so dearly. My family is always in front of my eyes and heart.

Look at Jerry, dressed as the clown he is, with the kids! I wonder how things might have been if he had come with a book of instructions.

Appendix III

THE FILMS OF JERRY LEWIS
(as compiled and critiqued by Scott Lewis.)

KEY: (1) = Actor; (2) = Director; (3) = Author;
(4) = Co-author; (5) = Producer

MY FRIEND IRMA (1)   *Paramount/1949*
Also starring Dean Martin. Co-starring: Marie Wilson, Don Defore, John Lund, Diane Lynn, Hans Conreid
This movie, based on a radio show of the same name, introduced Martin & Lewis to the big screen. M&L play aspiring performers who do odd jobs to get money to eat and generally cause all kinds of grief for the other players. My dad does a lot of the gags and mannerisms that made him famous.

MY FRIEND IRMA GOES WEST (1)   *Paramount/1950*
Also starring Dean Martin. Co-starring: Marie Wilson, Diane Lynn, John Lund, Corrine Calvet
The sequel was made as a result of the skyrocketing success of Martin & Lewis. Everyone dresses in western clothes and most of the comedy occurs on a train ride out west.

AT WAR WITH THE ARMY (1)   *Paramount/1951*
Also starring Dean Martin. Co-starring: Polly Bergen, Mike Kellin
The idea for this film came from a stage show. It proved

to be a terrific vehicle for M&L with Jerry as the scrawny private and Dean as his nasty sergeant. The most memorable scene is my dad "in drag," with a blonde wig and a low-cut dress showing his hairy chest.

THAT'S MY BOY (1)   *Paramount/1951*
Also starring Dean Martin. Co-starring: Ruth Hussey, Eddie Mayehoff, Marion Marshall, Polly Bergen, Tom Harmon
This film featured Eddie Mayehoff as "Jarring Jack Jackson," legendary ex-football star at the university. His son, Junior (Jerry) is not athletic and is kind of sickly, but his father persuades him to play football. Dean is his roommate and team-mate and they fight to win games and the same girl. My dad loved working with Eddie Mayehoff.

SAILOR BEWARE (1)   *Paramount/ 1952*
Also starring Dean Martin. Co-starring: Marion Marshall, Robert Strauss, Corinne Calvet
The boys wreak havoc on the navy this time. Some funny bits and some good songs. There is a great boxing sequence at the end of the picture in which my dad fights a man three times his size. In the big man's corner, as one of his trainers, is the as-yet-unknown James Dean.

JUMPING JACKS (1)   *Paramount/1952*
Also starring Dean Martin. Co-starring: Mona Freeman, Robert Strauss
In my opinion, this is the best military film my dad made. There are some hysterical scenes at the Fort Benning, Georgia, paratrooper training facility as the boys learn to jump out of planes. My dad even finds a way to win the war games for his side.

THE STOOGE (1)   *Paramount/1952*
Also starring Dean Martin. Co-starring: Polly Bergen, Eddie Mayehoff, Marion Marshall, Francis Bauvier
Martin & Lewis started to hit their stride in *Jumping*

Jacks, but in *The Stooge* they reached a full gallop. This is the story of a two-bit singer (Martin) who needs a stooge to make his act successful. Of course, he finds Jerry and the act is a smash success because of the comedy the little guy brings to each performance. It's really a very close parody to what occurred in their real-life careers. There are many memorable gags and songs. This is one of my favorites.

SCARED STIFF (1) *Paramount/1953*
Also starring Dean Martin. Co-starring: Lizabeth Scott, Dorothy Malone, Carmen Miranda

Most of the comedy occurs as the boys escort Lizabeth Scott to a haunted castle left to her in a will. Once again, this film is rich with sight gags and expressions of terror from my dad as he dodges ghosts and gangsters. There is a funny cameo at the end of the picture by Bob Hope and Bing Crosby, who appear as skeletons. (My dad and Dean also did a cameo in the Hope/Crosby picture *Road to Bali*. They all worked for Paramount.)

THE CADDY (1) *Paramount/1953*
Also starring Dean Martin. Co-starring: Donna Reed, Barbara Bates, Fred Clark, Tom Harmon, Marshall Thompson, Sam Snead, Ben Hogan

Dean is an aspiring pro golfer and Jerry is his friend and caddy who will do anything to further his friend's career. There is a great scene where my dad destroys the entire department store where he works. My dad also does a great imitation of a snobbish socialite. In real life, both men love golf passionately, so this film was a natural for them.

MONEY FROM HOME (1) *Paramount/1954*
Also starring Dean Martin. Co-starring: Patricia Crowley, Robert Strauss, Sheldon Leonard, Jack Kruschen, Richard Hadyn, Romo Vincent

This was the first color film for M&L. In it, my dad is a jockey who has to get by scores of gangsters who are trying to fix the big race in their favor. It's not their strongest comedy, but there is a funny scene where my dad dresses as an Arabian dancing girl and dances for a sheik.

LIVING IT UP (1)   *Paramount/1954*

Also starring Dean Martin. Co-starring: Janet Leigh, Fred Clark, Edward Arnold, Sheree North

This is the remake of the Carole Lombard classic, *Nothing Sacred*, about a person with a terminal illness who decides to have a final fling in the big city. My dad plays the doomed man who thinks he's dying of radiation poisoning. Dean is his doctor who accompanies him to New York for this final fling, courtesy of the local newspaper which wants to cover the story for its sympathetic readers. I think this remake is a classic in its own right. It is loaded with comedy and was beautifully photographed.

THREE RING CIRCUS (1)   *Paramount/1954*

Also starring Dean Martin. Co-starring: Zsa Zsa Gabor, Joanne Dru, Elsa Lanchester

The boys work in the circus as roustabouts but Jerry dreams of being a clown. When he finally gets the chance to perform in that capacity at a benefit for handicapped children, he walks over to a little girl with braces on her legs. He can't make her laugh and this upsets him so much, he begins to cry. With that, the little girl laughs and exclaims, "The clown is crying." Then my dad laughs, too. It could be the most touching moment of any of his films, especially in view of his work with Muscular Dystrophy.

YOU'RE NEVER TOO YOUNG (1)   *Paramount/1955*

Also starring Dean Martin. Co-starring: Raymond Burr, Diane Lynn, Nina Foch, Mitzi McCall

Raymond Burr is a gangster who is after Jerry because he has a jewel that Burr stole. To hide out, Jerry pretends he is a teenage boy and goes to live at an all-girl school where Dean is a teacher. The most memorable scene is at the beginning when Jerry tries his hand at being a barber with Dean as the guinea pig.

ARTISTS AND MODELS (1)   *Paramount/1955*

Also starring Dean Martin. Co-starring: Dorothy Malone, Eddie Mayehoff, Shirley MacLaine, Eva Gabor, Anita Ekberg, Jack Elam

This is another vehicle filled with gangsters. M&L play aspiring artists trying to make it big in the comic-book industry. It's not one of the most noteworthy pictures except for the fact that Shirley MacLaine made her film debut in it.

PARDNERS (1)   *Paramount/1956*

Also starring Dean Martin. Co-starring: Agnes Moorehead, Richard Aherne, Lon Chaney Jr., Jack Elam, Lee Van Cleef

In this picture M&L make the most of cowboy costumes. They do a little rodeo riding and some shooting. Not one of their best efforts, but it does have some funny moments. After seeing this picture, one might feel as if the studio was having a tough time finding a different sort of vehicle to put them in.

HOLLYWOOD OR BUST (1)   *Paramount/ 1956*

Also starring Dean Martin. Co-starring: Patricia Crowley, Anita Ekberg

Even though their partnership was almost at an end, Martin & Lewis went out with a bang. This is the story of two New Yorkers who both have the same winning ticket—Dean's printed bogusly—in a lottery for a new car. They decide to co-own the car and travel across the country to see Hollywood. My dad also takes along his very smart Great Dane, Mr. Baskim, who sees to it that Dean doesn't do anything underhanded to Jerry. It's a terrific movie. If I had to pick the best M&L movie, it would be a toss-up between *The Stooge, Living It Up,* or *Hollywood or Bust.* Regardless of their personal problems working together, I think these three movies should be the ones to go into a time capsule that would best represent the genius that was Martin & Lewis.

THE DELICATE DELINQUENT (1, 4, 5)   *Paramount/1957*
Co-starring: Darren McGavin, Martha Hyer, Robert Ivers
This proved to be a commercially successful vehicle for my dad as an individual star. In it, he plays a mild-mannered apartment house janitor who aspires to be a policeman. There are some funny moments and some serious messages about teenage delinquency. In the only song in the film my dad sings, "I'm by myself, alone."

THE SAD SACK (1, 3)   *Paramount/1958*
Co-starring: David Wayne, Phyllis Kirk, Peter Lorre, Michael Ansara
The plot of this picture had my father as the only munitions specialist who could assemble a highly secret piece of field artillery. Everyone is trying to kidnap him so they can own the assembled weapon. Peter Lorre plays an Arab who tries to kill my dad throughout the whole movie. The picture was shot in Yuma, Arizona, at the army base when I was two. I have some pictures of dad and me on that set.

ROCKABYE BABY (1, 4, 5)   *Paramount/1958*
Co-starring: Reginald Gardener, Connie Stevens, Marilyn Maxwell, Hans Conreid, Gary Lewis, James Gleason
Jerry has been unwittingly recruited to care for three little babies left on his doorstep. They are the children of his childhood sweetheart (Marilyn Maxwell), a movie star undertaking the role of The White Virgin of the Nile. Since it would be bad publicity for a "virgin" to have children, she leaves the children with him. This is a very heartwarming picture in which my dad dreams of when he was a boy. Next to him appears my brother, Gary, playing my father as a boy, and they sing a duet. Of course, it has a happy ending.

THE GEISHA BOY (1, 4, 5)   *Paramount/1958*
Co-starring: Suzanne Pleshette, Barton Maclane, Marie McDonald, Sessue Hayakawa

This is a beautiful story about a down-and-out magician and his truly magical rabbit, Harry, who go to Japan to entertain troops but fail at that. The magician meets a beautiful Japanese girl and her nephew and falls in love with both of them. There are a couple of parts in this movie that bring tears to my eyes every time I see it. This picture, along with *Rockabye Baby*, proves how multi-talented my dad is. In this movie, you laugh, you cry, and you enjoy every minute of it.

DON'T GIVE UP THE SHIP (1)   *Paramount/1959*
Co-starring: Claude Akins, Gale Gordon, Dina Merrill, Mickey Shaugnessy

This is not a great film. It is actually sort of ridiculous, having low production values and an unbelievable story line. My dad is a commander of a battleship which he seems to have misplaced.

VISIT TO A SMALL PLANET (1)   *Paramount/1960*
Co-starring: Fred Clark, Lee Patrick, Joan Blackman, Earl Holliman, Gale Gordon, John Williams, Ellen Corby, Buddy Rich

This picture was an adaptation of a Gore Vidal novel about a spaceman named Kryton, who was cohabitating with an Earth family. It was very loosely adapted for my father's specific talents. There are loads of sight gags and special effects, such as the alien visitor getting frustrated with traffic on the freeway, levitating his car and flying above everyone else. He is also equipped with an invisible barrier which protects him from harm. It's a very entertaining movie.

THE BELLBOY (1, 2, 3, 5)   *Paramount/1960*
Co-starring: Bob Clayton, Milton Berle

My dad was growing by leaps and bounds when it came to his knowledge of film-making. Paramount agreed to let him direct and produce *The Bellboy*. However, he was already committed to do *Cinderfella* and had only a small window of time to complete every facet of *The Bellboy*. My dad went to the Fountainbleu Hotel in Miami Beach and made comedic history. In just six weeks he shot a movie that was made up of vignettes and, I think, ranks as one of his best films. We simply followed my dad (Stanley, the bellboy) through his daily routine at the hotel. He doesn't even speak until the final scene, when a lady pulls up in a Volkswagen Beetle (a rear-engine car) and asks Stanley to bring up everything in her trunk... so, of course, the engine is brought to her room. I will always love this movie because I was there for a lot of the filming. I had an unforgettable birthday party at the hotel and when I lived in Florida for three years at the end of the eighties, I had occasion to go to the Fountainbleu where a lot of nice memories came back.

CINDERFELLA (1, 5)   *Paramount/1960*
Co-starring: Dame Judith Anderson, Ed Wynn, Henry Silva, Robert Hutton, Anna Maria Alberghetti, Joe Williams, Count Basie and Orchestra
This is the traditional story of Cinderella with my dad as the hero named Fella. His stepmother and stepbrothers are nasty to him until his fairy godfather (Ed Wynn) helps him. Fella sings "Let me be a people," which is a reference to the fact that he feels less than human. It's touching and funny and it also has the traditional happy ending. The Kirkeby Estate in Bel Air—also home to the Beverly Hillbillies—was used as the family mansion for exterior shots. I remember being on that set and in one scene, the family fortune of coins and jewels was laid out in a wheelbarrow. My dad gave us a few of the "coins" to eat. They were foil-covered chocolate and showed us at a very early age that the movies were a world of make-believe.

THE LADIES' MAN (1, 2, 4, 5)   *Paramount/1961*
Co-starring: Helen Traubel, Kathleen Freeman, George Raft, Doodles Weaver, Buddy Lester, Harry James and Orchestra

This is the story of a young man who has been jilted by his girlfriend and can't bear even being around women. He takes a job as a houseman, not realizing it is in a women-only rooming house. There are innumerable gags. One of my favorites is when George Raft comes to the house to pick up his date. While he waits, he talks to my dad, who doesn't believe him, but admits the real Raft would be a terrific dancer because he did a lot of dancing in his pictures. The music comes up, the lights dim, the spotlight comes on, and they dance around the living room together. It's really great. The set of the rooming house that was built for that picture was then the most expensive set ever built for any movie. It cost $1 million, had three stories and took up two complete sound stages. I remember being on that set, too, and it was absolutely magnificent.

IT'S ONLY MONEY (1, 5)   *Paramount/1962*
Co-starring: Zachary Scott, Jesse White, Jack Weston, Mae Questal

This film has my dad playing a mild-mannered TV repairman who does not realize he is heir to a fortune. The people who guard that secret are trying to kill him off so they can keep the fortune themselves. This picture has too much story line and not enough comedy for my dad to do. I recall being on this set and being amazed at how unrealistic everything looked in person. That is true with every movie, but I was still at a very impressionable age and didn't understood much about movie-making.

THE ERRAND BOY (1, 2, 4, 5)   *Paramount/1962*
Co-starring: Brian Donlevy, Howard McNear

This is perhaps one of the funniest of my father's movies, and because it's about movie making, it holds a special place in my heart. It has a little more story than *The Bellboy*, but not much. My dad has a field day as an unwitting "kid" who is hired by the studio to sniff out cost overruns. There are classic scenes all through it. This movie could be put in a time capsule and everyone who sees it would see everything Jerry Lewis excelled at on film. This movie has fantasy, slapstick, pantomime, facial expressions, and overall genius. It has to be seen to be believed.

THE NUTTY PROFESSOR (1, 2, 4, 5)   *Paramount/1963*

Co-starring: Stella Stevens, Del Moore, Kathleen Freeman, Howard Morris, Elvia Allman, Henry Gibson, Med Flory, Les Brown and his Band of Renown

When people talk about the films of Jerry Lewis, invariably *The Nutty Professor* is mentioned first. It is the classic tale of Dr. Jekyll and Mr. Hyde. Mild-mannered Professor Julius Kelp is tired of being pushed around, so he turns to chemistry, his field of expertise, for the solution to his problems. Instead of strengthening his body, the formula alters his personality—he becomes the extroverted, conceited, and snobbish Buddy Love. The vicious cycle continues until finally he undergoes a metamorphosis from Buddy back to Julius in front of the entire student body. This film takes some of my dad's funniest talents and enhances them even more with a terrific story. Playing a nasty, chauvinistic character who even beats up a guy in one scene was quite a change of pace for Dad. I remember the shock of being on the set and in the presence of whatever character my dad was playing that day. As Julius, he had funny hair and buck teeth. As Buddy, he looked almost effeminate, with eye-liner and greased-back hair. My mom remembers that the characters he portrayed during the day affected his mood when he came home. My brothers and I were not allowed to see that movie until we were teenagers; Mom did not want us to see our father as Buddy. The movie is unique— whether it's being discussed by a comedy or horror-film aficionado, it is considered a classic.

WHO'S MINDING THE STORE? (1)   *Paramount/1963*

Co-starring: Agnes Moorehead, Jill St. John, John McGiver, Ray Walston, Nancy Kulp, Fritz Feld

Just imagine anything that could go wrong in a

department store and you have the premise for this film, which really is terrific. In the gourmet department, Dad is forced to eat disgusting "foreign" foods. A lady wrestler attacks him in the shoe department. In sporting goods he destroys a golf machine and shoots off a shotgun. In appliances, he fixes a vacuum cleaner so well that it sucks up everything, including a patron's dog. And in one of my favorite scenes he's the clerk in the bargain basement. Women going for bargains are depicted as sharks going for red meat as they pour in and grab for everything, including the clerk's clothes. The movie also has a love story and, of course, a happy ending.

THE PATSY (1, 2, 4, 5)   *Paramount/1964*
Co-starring: Keenan Wynn, Phil Harris, Ina Balin, Everett Sloane, Peter Lorre, John Carradine, Hans Conreid, Richard Deacon, Scatman Crothers, Neil Hamilton, Nancy Kulp, Lloyd Thaxton, Jack Albertson, Ned Wynn, Rhonda Fleming, Phil Foster, Hedda Hopper, George Raft, Ed Sullivan, The Step Brothers, Mel Torme, Ed Wynn, Jerry Dunphy

The death of a world-famous comedian leaves his entourage in a quandary. If they don't find a substitute superstar, their credibility will be gone and they will be out of work. My dad is a hapless bellboy who comes up to their room and is drafted for stardom. This picture does have a lot of funny moments, but it never really gels as one of Dad's best efforts.

THE DISORDERLY ORDERLY (1, 5)   *Paramount/1964*
Co-starring: Susan Oliver, Karen Sharp, Glenda Farrell, Del Moore, Everett Sloane, Kathleen Freeman, Alice Pierce Jack Leonard

Another true *tour de force*. The jokes just keep mounting. Every time I see it, I like it more. Dad is an orderly who spends every day making life miserable for head nurse Kathleen Freeman (a dear friend of mine), at a mental institution. The comedy is so diverse, it is enjoyable throughout. At the end of the movie, there is a wacky ambulance chase and a couple of runaway stretchers.

THE FAMILY JEWELS (1, 2, 3, 5)   *Paramount/1965*
Co-starring: Donna Butterworth, Neil Hamilton, Sebastian Cabot, Robert Strauss, Ellen Corby, Anne Baxter

Donna Butterworth is a little girl whose millionaire father has just died. In the will it's stipulated that she spend time with each of her uncles then decide who will be her guardian and in control of her father's millions. Of course, each uncle is played by my father. He is also Willard, the chauffeur. The funniest uncle is the gangster, Bugsy, who wants Donna for the money and kidnaps her, forcing the other uncles to band together for her rescue. It is a marvelous showcase for the many faces of Jerry Lewis. We stopped at the set on the way to Disneyland for my birthday celebration and Dad, dressed as Uncle Julius, stopped everything so everyone could sing "Happy Birthday" to me. After posing for some pictures, we were again on the way. Events such as that caused me to grow up feeling very comfortable on a movie set. Dad used to hurry home after the last shot of the day, still dressed in the costume of whatever character he had been portraying, so he could watch the dailies (footage shot the day before) in our living room. I sat beside him as he explained why a shot was good or bad and what he had to do to correct it. Even though I was only about nine, I was always fascinated.

BOEING, BOEING (1)   *Paramount/1965*
Co-starring: Tony Curtis, Thelma Ritter

This movie was made to fulfill the studio contract and is probably one of the worst he has ever been in. At least he can't be blamed for bad directing or producing. The story revolves around Tony Curtis who has three live-in stewardess girlfriends. They all travel at different times and are unaware of each other. Dad is a friend of Tony's and wants to hang around in case a little action swings his way. There's a scene in the movie where Dad is brutally beaten and I can remember how that upset me as a kid.

THREE ON A COUCH (1, 2, 3, 5)   *Columbia/1966*
Co-starring: Janet Leigh, James Best, Mary Ann Mobley, Gila Golan, Leslie Parrish, Renzo Cesana, Fritz Feld, Kathleen Freeman

In this movie, Dad is an artist who wins an award to work in Paris. His girlfriend, Janet Leigh, is a psychologist with three female patients who have nothing but trouble with the men in their lives. She feels she can't go to Paris until her patients start to get better. To speed things up, Dad impersonates a perfect match for each of these women and they start to have improved sessions. My favorite part is when Dad plays a Southern belle with red hair. There are a few laughs, but that's about it.

WAY, WAY OUT (1)   *20th Century-Fox/1966*
Co-starring: John Morley, Connie Stevens, Howard Morris, Dennis Weaver, Dick Shawn, Brian Keith, James Brolin

Dad and Connie Stevens wed in order to be the first married couple on the moon. The most memorable thing about this movie is Dick Shawn playing a visiting Russian cosmonaut. When the movie came out, 20th provided our entire family with spacesuits like the ones worn by Dad in the movie and we all wore them to a press party at the studio.

THE BIG MOUTH (1, 2, 4, 5)   *Columbia/1967*
Co-starring: Susan Bay, Leonard Stone, Charlie Callas, Harold Stone, Buddy Lester, Del Moore, Colonel Sanders

A gangster dies in my father's arms and his enemies think he's confided the location of a fortune in stolen diamonds. About the best thing here are the numerous disguises Dad uses to escape. A number of the scenes were shot on the beach at Malibu. I almost got sunstroke from being in the intense sun all day.

DON'T RAISE THE BRIDGE, LOWER THE RIVER (1, 5)   *Columbia/1968*
Co-starring: Terry Thomas, Jaquiline Pearce, Jerry Paris
This picture, directed by Jerry Paris and shot in London,

was so bad and it has been so long since seeing it, I can't even remember what it was about.

HOOK, LINE AND SINKER (1, 5)   *Columbia/1969*
Co-starring: Peter Lawford, Ann Francis
In this, Dad is married to Ann Francis. Peter Lawford is their doctor who convinces Dad to fake his own death to collect the insurance. The doctor, however, has his own designs on Miss Francis. This forgettable film was partially shot in Portugal.

ONE MORE TIME (2)   *1969*
Starring: Peter Lawford, Sammy Davis, Jr. Co-starring: John Wood, Christopher Lee, Peter Cushing
Dad directed this sequel to *Salt and Pepper*. The strange, mysterious goings-on in an old English mansion call for the skill of detectives Salt and Pepper. In one scene, the script called for Sammy, who was deathly afraid of heights, to walk down a stairway facing the camera, only to be greeted by vampire Christopher Lee and the mad doctor Peter Cushing in the basement. He could barely do the scene. But what fun it was for me meeting two of the great horror film stars. Even though Mr. Lee showed us how he made his eyes red with drops, I have to admit it was impossible to look cool standing next to him. My family and I spent over two months in England while the movie was being shot in and around London. While there, we watched the moon landing of our astronauts on a giant movie screen set up in Trafalgar Square.

WHICH WAY TO THE FRONT? (1, 2, 4, 5)
Warner Brothers/1970
Co-starring: Jan Murray, Willie Davis, Steve Franken, Dack Rambo, John Wood, Sidney Miller, Paul Winchell, Kaye Ballard, Robert Middleton, George Takai, Joe Besser, Mickey Manners, Neil Hamilton, Benny Rubin, Gary Crosby, Don Sutton, Ron Lewis
A millionaire, declared 4-F when he wants to enlist to fight Nazis, rounds up a bunch of other 4-Fs and finances

his own army. I think the most memorable things about this movie are my dad playing Field Marshall Kesslering, with a very funny Kaye Ballard as his mistress, and Sidney Miller's portrayal of Hitler. On this set I formed a close and lasting affection for Jan Murray—Uncle Jan, even today. He is a very sweet man and a true genius when it comes to comedy.

THE DAY THE CLOWN CRIED (1, 2, 3)   *Unreleased/1971*
Dad went from doing a lampoon of World War II to a serious drama about it. He plays Helmut, a German Jew who is a real clown in the circus. Arrested one night for drunkenly speaking against Hitler, he is thrown in a concentration camp where he survives by entertaining the soldiers and keeping the Jewish children from crying. After terrible persecutions by the Germans, he is ordered to guide the children into the gas chamber. As he stands outside watching, a little girl who has become special to him reaches for his hand and he elects to walk in with her. As the door closes, we hear the sound of hissing gas as the camera pulls away. Arguments with the producer kept the film from ever being completed or released. That was a tremendous disappointment for Dad, who had put so much of his soul into the project. I will never forget the impression it made on me the one time we saw the rough cut. Dad was so soured by this experience that he didn't do another movie for the next eight years, seeking every other type of work instead. I would have loved to have seen this film finished. It could have ranked up there with other classics such as Charlie Chaplin's *The Great Dictator*.

HARDLY WORKING (1, 2, 4)   *20th Century Fox/1981*
Co-starring: Susan Oliver, Roger C. Carmel, Harold Stone, Steve Franken, Leonard Stone, Diana Lund, Billy Barty
This is about a guy who can't hold a job. He tries everything from being a postal worker to a clown and nothing is right. Working with Dad on this film in Florida

was my closest experience to making a movie. Halfway through, a new producer had to be brought in. Under great pressure, (he was still smoking heavily and his marriage was about to end) Dad looks awful in the film. His face is drawn and ashen, his eyes are red. Even though the movie has so much going against it, there are a few funny scenes that are vintage Jerry Lewis. Every time I see it, it's like watching home movies of summer camp because I was there for practically every shot, unless I was running errands. In fact, I met my first wife during the filming.

THE KING OF COMEDY (1)   *20th Century Fox/1981*
Co-starring: Robert DeNiro, Sandra Bernhard, Diane Abbott, Shelly Hack, Fred De Cordova, Tony Randall, Dr. Joyce Brothers
In this picture, directed by Martin Scorsese, Dad plays a true-to-life character—Jerry Langford, famous comedian and talk show host, idolized and emulated by DeNiro. After several fruitless attempts to communicate with his idol, DeNiro and Bernhard kidnap Jerry. A lot of people hail this as a masterpiece, but as an actor Dad was not challenged enough. I think it showed the public what celebrity life is really like, to some extent, and what it takes to protect yourself from threats and maintain some semblance of privacy.

SLAPSTICK (1)   *Columbia/1982*
Co-starring: Madeline Kahn, Marty Feldman, Pat Morita
Directed by a young man in his twenties, Steven Paul, this project was totally botched. Dad and Madeline Kahn have dual roles as earthlings and grotesque aliens. It was so awful I could not even make it to the end.

CRACKING UP (1, 2, 4)   *Warner Brothers/1982*
Co-starring: Herb Edleman, Dick Butkus, Ben Davidson, Foster Brooks, Milton Berle, Sammy Davis Jr., Zane Busby
I got my first executive credit as associate producer on this film, in which Dad plays an anxiety-ridden man who keeps trying to kill himself because he thinks it's impossible

to succeed and seeks help from his psychologist. Once again, the pressure to bring the film in on time and under budget was terrible. Neither happened. Dad was only months away from his heart bypass surgery and did not look good. This is a fairly depressing movie, lacking many jokes. The funniest scene is with Milton Berle in drag trying to hit on Dad in the psychologist's office.

Since *Cracking Up,* Dad has had a few small roles and a leading role in a TV movie. He also has done two or three foreign productions which I have not yet seen.